The Drug Industry

The Canadian Institute for Economic Policy has been established to engage in public discussion of fiscal, industrial and other related public policies designed to strengthen Canada in a rapidly changing international environment.

The Institute fulfills this mandate by sponsoring and undertaking studies pertaining to the economy of Canada and disseminating such studies. Its intention is to contribute in an innovative way to the development of public policy in Canada.

Canadian Institute for Economic Policy
Suite 409, 350 Sparks St., Ottawa K1R 7S8

The Drug Industry

A Case Study in Foreign Control

Myron J. Gordon and David J. Fowler

James Lorimer & Company, Publishers
in association with the
Canadian Institute for Economic Policy
Toronto 1981

Copyright © 1981 by Canadian Institute for Economic Policy

ISBN 0-88862-536-7 cloth
ISBN 0-88862-535-9 paper

6 5 4 3 2 1   81 82 83 84 85 86

Canadian Cataloguing in Publication Data

Gordon, Myron J.
  The drug industry

ISBN 0-88862-536-7 (bound). - ISBN 0-88862-537-5 (university). - ISBN 0-88862-535-9 (pbk.)

1. Drug trade - Canada. 2. Business enterprises, Foreign - Canada. I. Fowler, David John.   II. Canadian Institute for Economic Policy. III. Title.

HD9670.C22G67   338.4'36151'0971   C81-095085-5

C. 1

38, 901

Additional copies of this book
may be purchased from:

James Lorimer & Company, Publishers
Egerton Ryerson Memorial Building
35 Britain Street
Toronto M5A 1R7, Ontario

Printed and bound in Canada

Contents

Tables

Foreword

Canada is unique among industrialized countries in the level of foreign ownership of its economy. The consequences of foreign ownership of firms are now well known: the Canadian subsidiary usually has a truncated form of operations, has limited linkages to Canadian suppliers, is import-intensive and has little propensity to export, since it was established to serve the Canadian market. Because they exhibit such characteristics, foreign-owned firms do not serve Canada well.

As the authors indicate, the behaviour of the pharmaceutical industry in Canada is in keeping with that of other foreign-dominated sectors. Moreover, Drs. Gordon and Fowler indicate that it will be difficult to increase the level of Canadian ownership, given the nature of the industry and the market power of the multinational firms.

The Institute is publishing this study to stimulate public discussion of the consequences of foreign control of our economy. As with all our studies, the views expressed here are those of the authors and do not necessarily reflect those of the Institute.

Roger Voyer
Executive Director
Canadian Institute for Economic Policy

Acknowledgements

Our motivation for this study was an interest in the questions pertaining to foreign ownership and to a strategy for the development of Canadian industry. We believed that the most effective way to explore these questions was to look at one industry in some detail, but prior knowledge of the pharmaceutical industry was certainly not one of the considerations that led to its selection for our study. In fact, our knowledge of the pharmaceutical industry at the inception of this study was not perceptibly greater than the information one might gain by patronizing one's neighbourhood drug store.

Whatever knowledge we have acquired of the industry is in large measure due to the many industry and government people who gave so generously of their time in response to our requests for information. Their generosity was all the more striking since it was clear to many of them that they might not be happy with our conclusions. It follows that the specific recognition below of persons who have been exceptionally generous of their time does not imply their endorsement of this study. We are especially grateful to Mr. Leslie Dan of Novopharm; Mr. Don Davies of Ayerst, McKenna and Harrison; Mr. E. D. Ellis and Dr. Fenton Hay of the Department of Consumer and Corporate Affairs, Ottawa; Mr. R. Everson of Pharmaceutical Manufacturers Association of Canada; Dr. J. K. W. Ferguson, formerly of Connaught Laboratories; Mr. Brian King of CDC (Canada Development Corporation) Life Sciences; and Mr. Percy Skuy of Ortho Pharmaceutical (Canada) Limited.

This study would not have been possible without the research environment provided by the Faculty of Management Studies, University of Toronto, and the Faculty of Management, McGill University. We are also grateful to the Canadian Institute for Economic Policy for their financial support and to Walter Gordon and Abraham Rotstein of the CIEP for their belief in the importance of this study.

Contact with these two men was a unique education in how to combine humanism, common sense and nationalism in confronting public policy issues—and in having a great time in the process.

Mr. Warren Bailey conscientiously carried out the onerous task of developing our price indices. Mrs. Linda Palanica of the Faculty of Management Studies, University of Toronto, and Mrs. Sandy Grew of the Faculty of Management, McGill University, cheerfully typed and retyped many drafts of the manuscript. Finally, whatever success we have achieved in communicating what was in our minds is due to the gifted and tireless editorial work of Mrs. Betty Gordon.

The Problem of Foreign Ownership and Control

1

A striking feature of the Canadian economy is the extraordinary degree to which markets in Canada for high-technology, manufactured products are satisfied by foreign corporations through some combination of exports to Canada and subsidiary production in Canada. The extent of foreign ownership and control is well documented; readily available statistics show that Canadian subsidiaries of foreign corporations have 70 to 80 per cent, or more, of the sales, assets and profits of a large number of important, high-technology Canadian industries.

However, although the extent of foreign ownership and control is readily acknowledged, there are widely differing conclusions on what the economic and political consequences are for Canada and on what government policy should be with regard to the problem and to related questions of industrial strategy. The diversity of opinion on these matters is due in large measure to the limited evidence on the consequences of foreign ownership and to the tendency to consider the problem for the manufacturing sector as a whole rather than for each industry separately.

This study examines the performance of the Canadian pharmaceutical industry and the government's alternative policy options for it. Drug manufacturing was selected because it has a high level of technology, a high degree of foreign ownership, and good comparative data. A standard of performance is established that is quite general, and the performance of the industry is evaluated on the basis of this standard and the available data. The desirability of each of the policy options open to the federal and provincial governments depends on the organization, structure and other attributes of the drug industry, both here and abroad. This study endeavours to establish these attributes, as well as the industry's performance statistics, in order to reach sound conclusions on optimal policy for the industry. It is hoped that the study will prove useful as a guide for government policy. Although the policy conclusions reached cannot be applied mechanically to other industries, the method of analysis should be useful for studying other industries in the manufacturing sector.

Positions on Foreign Ownership
Multinationalist Position

The multinationalist position on foreign ownership is that subsidiaries here are a means of transferring technology to Canada. The implication is that "technology transfer" makes available to Canada the finest products at the lowest possible prices while providing Canadians with the employment required to satisfy the demand for the industry's products.[1] The alternatives to the presence of the multinational subsidiaries are either to import foreign products in finished form or to have Canadian firms do the manufacturing. Imports provide Canada with foreign products at the same prices that prevail in the home country—plus a transportation charge—but that charge is ordinarily quite small for high-technology products. However, imports do deny Canadians the attractive employment opportunities that go with meeting the demand for high-technology products. The employment problem could be solved by restricting the market to firms that are owned domestically, but the claim is that when multinational firms are kept out of the Canadian market by government intervention instead of by the free play of competition, the result is inferior products and higher costs than would otherwise prevail.

The term "technology transfer" is central to the above characterization of what multinational corporations bring to a country. Therefore, a precise definition of the term is desirable. Technology transfer is said to take place when the methods of manufacture developed in one country are transferred to another country. The benefits attributed to multinational corporations suggest another definition of the term *and it furnishes the theoretical basis for this study*: technology transfer takes place *completely* when a foreign subsidiary in Canada (1) sells its parent company's products in Canada at prices comparable to those charged in the parent country, and (2) provides a market in Canada for employees, materials and services that is comparable to the market provided by the parent company at home. That is, if the subsidiary's sales in Canada are 10 per cent of the parent's total sales, then the subsidiary is a correspondingly scaled-down version of the parent in terms of level and types of employment, rates of employment

2

compensation, market for raw materials, market for various business services, and business taxes. Notice that even with complete technology transfer, the profit on the capital employed (typically greater than a competitive return on capital) would still flow abroad. Complete technology transfer is, however, an impractical goal, like a perfect vacuum in physics or a perfectly competitive market in economic theory. Furthermore, policies of the parent company may not be the sole determinant of the extent to which technology transfer takes place, since the extent to which it *can* take place may be influenced considerably by differences between Canada and the parent country in size, degree of economic development, and governmental policies.

In summary, then, the multinationalist position is that in the absence of intervention by the Canadian government foreign subsidiaries will provide the technology transfer that is optimal in terms of product prices and domestic employment. The claim is that a higher degree of technology transfer would leave the Canadian economy worse off, as would sole reliance on imports or sole reliance on domestic firms.

Nationalist Position

Nationalists oppose foreign ownership on a number of grounds, including the flow of profits abroad and the loss of intangible benefits that national ownership of industry afford. However, their primary argument is that any technology transfer resulting from foreign ownership is so low that the elimination or substantial reduction of such ownership would materially improve Canada's economic welfare. They go on to argue that the commanding position of foreign multinational corporations in high-technology industries is due not to their better performance in serving Canada, but to their acquisitions, patents, predatory pricing, marketing practices and other instruments of monopoly power. It is the nationalist position that the industries dominated by multinationals are, in fact, characterized by a large number of small plants that use inefficient methods of production and limit their production either to the final assembly of components or to the mixing of ingredients—with the production of components/ingredients taking place abroad. In addition, much of a subsidiary's product line is imported as finished products. The nationalists maintain that as a result of these various practices the level of employment in Canada and its skill content are seriously reduced by foreign ownership.

When the financially rewarding and intellectually stimulating employment in managerial and professional activities is considered, nationalists claim that the performance of Canadian subsidiaries compares even less favourably with that of the parent companies. The Gray Report[2] characterized subsidiary corporations as "truncated" branch plants because their role is confined to the limited production described above, to sales and to their immediate supervision. Top management responsibilities and staff functions—such as investment decisions, research and development (R&D), market research, and systems development—remain abroad. It is further claimed that these truncated plants are also prohibited from serving export markets and from introducing new products initially into Canada.

The nationalist view that economic power—not economic efficiency—is the reason why foreign subsidiaries dominate high-technology industry in Canada leads to the conclusion that the powers of government should be used to reduce foreign ownership or eliminate it completely.[3]

Pragmatist Position

What may be called the pragmatist position is reflected in the tariff policy that has been followed by all Canadian governments, more or less, since 1879, that is, reliance on tariffs and other broad instruments of commercial policy to discourage—but not prohibit—the import of manufactured products. A century ago the tariff was the major source of federal revenues, and the bulk of these revenues was used to finance construction of the transcontinental railway—effectively the backbone of the country. Also, the tariff was seen to have several long-run, related benefits:

- domestic manufacture would be established, creating a demand for transportation of goods on the newly created railway system;
- domestic industry would be encouraged, leading to a better balance in railway transportation (grain moving east and manufactured goods going west);
- railway revenues would be increased, reducing the need for subsidies and lessening the demand for federal revenues.

This remarkably pragmatic and coherent tariff policy was based on economic nationalism and remained in place for fifty years.[4]

In more recent years the tariff has been retained on the ground that the domestic manufacturing made possible by a moderate tariff provides employment benefits that outweigh the higher production costs, while domestic production of goods that come in over the tariff would involve costs that outweigh the employment benefits.

The pragmatist position originally ignored the question of foreign ownership, for when governmental policy was established in the nineteenth century, the only material consequence of foreign ownership was the flow of profits abroad, a small price to pay at that time for the economic development made possible by the import of foreign capital. Until well after the First World War production was practically the sole activity of manufacturing firms in Canada, and the modest management structure required to supervise production was located at the production facility. The dramatic developments in communications, travel and the techniques of decentralized management, however, during the twentieth century, particularly since the end of the Second World War, have radically changed the nature of manufacturing firms. Now, large multinational corporations dominate manufacturing and engage in a wide range of managerial and professional activities in order to increase their profitability, activities that need not be carried on at the production facility. It is the ability of multinationals to manage truncated foreign subsidiaries that has added a new dimension to the question of foreign ownership.

In recent years the basically pragmatic policies of the federal government have been giving some recognition to the problems posed by the separation of production from the managerial and professional activities of the modern corporation. For some time this recognition was confined to special studies and data collection, with the latter including industry statistics on ownership, R&D and payments abroad for business services. Presumably the benefits of technology transfer and the problems involved in trying to reduce foreign ownership persuaded the government to move with extreme caution in changing its long-standing policy of indifference to foreign ownership.

What appears now to be emerging slowly in government, in sections of the business community, and in other circles is a modern version of the cautious, pragmatic nationalism of the nineteenth century: that is, the free and unfettered play of market forces in determining the presence and operation of multinational corporations in Canada may not be in the country's best interest. However, an immediate, massive reduction in foreign ownership is recognized as being highly undesirable—if not impossible. The practical alternative that is emerging consists of policies that would restrict growth in foreign ownership, maximize the benefits to Canada of the continued presence of multinational corporations, and reduce foreign ownership where the benefits are compelling.[5]

5

Free-Trade Position

The last major position on foreign ownership, termed here the free-trade position, is that foreign ownership is a non-issue. This position is held by those who believe that the neoclassical theory of a perfectly competitive economic system is a satisfactory description of the world economy in which Canada functions.[6] They are termed free-traders because free trade and the irrelevance of ownership both follow logically from the assumption that the markets, both here and abroad, for all products and for all factors of production are perfectly competitive.

The assumption of a perfectly competitive market requires, among other things:

- that the number of buyers and sellers of a product be so large that the price becomes independent of any one participant's purchases or sales;
- that each participant (consumer or producer) be completely informed on the quality and price—both present and future—of every product;
- that there be no transaction costs, meaning by this that a person can buy and sell the same house a hundred times without incurring any expense in the process.

Perhaps more important, the free-trade position not only requires that all product markets be perfectly competitive, it also requires that labour markets be perfectly competitive. In the latter event, full employment would be no problem, and differences in wage rates among occupations would only be due to differences in the pleasantness of the occupations and/or to differences in the cost of acquiring skills. In other words, no useful purpose would be served by policies to increase the level of employment or to increase the attractiveness and the pay scales of the available job opportunities. It should be noted that this view contrasts sharply with the popular wisdom that unemployment and the quality of job opportunities (for example, professional occupations versus unskilled manual jobs) are important concerns of public policy.

If markets throughout the world were perfectly competitive, free trade would result in international specialization and exchange so as to minimize production costs and maximize real income. Foreign ownership would not be an issue, because the only benefit from ownership would be the return on capital and that return would be everywhere the same. Consequently, it would be immaterial whether the capital a person owned was physically located at home or abroad. The location of managerial and professional activity would also not be an issue in a perfectly competitive system, since firms in such a system would not engage in these activities.

Free-traders argue further that government intervention (through tariffs and other instruments of commercial policy) comprises the only significant violation of perfect competition in the world. Like the nationalists, they find Canadian manufacturing to be highly inefficient, but they attribute this inefficiency solely to government interference, not to foreign ownership. They conclude that free trade or a customs union with the United States would have no adverse consequences for Canadian employment. Rather, free trade would replace the many small and inefficient plants that now characterize the Canadian manufacturing scene, with efficient, world-scale plants.[7]

Measurement of Industrial Performance
Theoretical Basis

Apart from those who support the free-trade position on foreign ownership, there is general agreement on how the performance of a Canadian subsidiary of a foreign multinational corporation should be judged. The lower the prices charged and the greater the level and skill content of the employment provided, the better the performance. Both of these dimensions of performance were incorporated in our definition of technology transfer that was suggested earlier. Establishing the degree to which a Canadian subsidiary enjoys the benefits of technology transfer *should* be a relatively straightforward task. From the records of a foreign multinational and its Canadian subsidiary, one should be able to obtain and analyze the relevant information (for example, prices charged, sales volume, level of employment, types of employment, rates of compensation, material purchases at home and abroad, and taxes paid) to determine the extent to which the subsidiary enjoys the parent's technology. Unfortunately, however, such data is not publicly reported. The annual reports and other information made public by parent and subsidiary companies contain very little pertinent information.

Much of the required data is provided to the statistical agencies of government in Canada and the U.S., but it is published by these agencies on an industry-wide basis only. Furthermore, some of the data provided is lost in aggregation. Nevertheless, what is published may be used in a comparative evaluation of the performance of an industry in the two countries. If the Canadian industry is largely owned by U.S. corporations, this comparison provides information on the extent to which technology transfer has taken place.

The above approach to the measurement of performance leads quite naturally to an industrial strategy for which the objectives are the lowest possible prices for the products of industry and the highest possible rates of compensation for the labour, capital and other resources employed by industry. If the quality of products and the pace at which desirable new products are introduced depend on the industrial strategy pursued, then they also are matters of concern. These objectives are largely in conflict with each other in a *closed* economy, where the mix of products produced is determined by the domestic demand for output, and the means for producing the output are confined to domestic labour, capital and management. In fact, for a closed economy lower prices for products and higher rates of compensation for the factors employed by industry can only be achieved through policies that increase productivity. In an *open* economy, however, the policy alternatives for realizing the goals of industrial strategy are greatly expanded. Exports and imports make the bill of goods produced independent of the bill of goods consumed. In addition, foreign ownership and management of industry are alternatives to their domestic counterparts. Hence, both trade and foreign control of industry may either serve or harm society, and both are proper concerns of industrial strategy.

Previous Literature

There is considerable literature devoted to the performance of the Canadian manufacturing sector and to comparing it with manufacturing in the U.S. However, as noted earlier, most of this literature examines the problem under the assumption of perfect competition, and this leads to a free-trade conclusion. The question of foreign ownership seems to be studiously ignored, causing one economist to comment:

> Rather, the pervasive presence of foreign direct investment gives one cause to be puzzled that so much macro-economic analysis and policy prescription have been forthcoming in Canada with little realistic recognition of the special circumstances and problems that this investment has produced.[8]

Furthermore, empirical work in the area is largely confined to industries with simple product lines, probably so as to increase data accuracy when comparing Canadian and American productivity and price levels. But in such industries technology and foreign ownership are relatively low.[9]

Perhaps the most influential work in support of free trade has been a book by Wonnacott and Wonnacott that predicted in 1966 (using 1958 data) that free trade would increase Canada's gross national product (GNP) by 10.5 per cent.[10] This would take place, according to the authors, through the elimination of those industries for which Canada has a comparative disadvantage, and through both the expansion and the rise in productivity to U.S. levels of those industries for which Canada has a comparative advantage. The data presented by the authors to support their predicted 10.5 per cent increase in the GNP was quite sketchy, but one gets the impression that their conclusion was based largely on the belief that labour productivity in manufacturing would increase by about 20 per cent.

Of course, the immediate impact of free trade would be a sharp deterioration in the competitive position of the manufacturing sector in Canada as a whole, since the inefficiency of its existing industry makes Canadian prices substantially higher than U.S. prices. However, this deterioration did not trouble the Wonnacotts, and they did not foresee any unemployment problems other than the time required to retrain and relocate workers affected by the liquidation of some industries. How did they reach their conclusion that employment in manufacturing would be maintained and that productivity would rise quickly to U.S. levels? They assumed reasonably that a plant in Canada with the same equipment, the same product line, and the same production schedule as a U.S. plant would have the same labour productivity. They then determined that in some industries the Canadian plant would have roughly 5 per cent lower production costs—due primarily to lower wage rates—and this would certainly lead, they argued, to a rapid and massive increase in world-scale manufacturing plants in Canada. This conclusion on the movement of industry to Canada in response to modest differences in production costs is highly questionable.

Nonetheless, assume with the Wonnacotts that free trade would replace Canada's present manufacturing plants with world-scale plants—comparable in productivity to those in the U.S. and specializing in industries according to the law of comparative advantage. Their conclusion that the gain resulting from the increased productivity would remain in Canada is based on two grossly incorrect assumptions: (1) that the value of an industry's output is equal to the

9

cost of producing the output; and (2) that an increase in productivity increases a country's GNP by the amount of the increase. With regard to the first assumption, in a perfectly competitive system the value of an industry's output would be completely accounted for by its costs of production—material cost, production wages, depreciation on capital, and a fair pretax return on capital. In reality, though, the value of its output also includes any profits that are in excess of a fair pretax return on capital and, of more importance, the costs of those nonproduction persons—clerical, professional and managerial—who are either employed directly by the firm or are employed in providing the services purchased by the firm. In high-technology industries these other shares in the value of output can be very large, as much as four times the wages of production workers, as will be seen later. With regard to the second assumption, the replacement in Canada of a number of small and inefficient plants with one world-scale plant would require the transfer of production workers and some low-level salaried employees. However, the remainder of the salaried employment and most of the gain from the increased productivity would quite likely flow abroad—not remain in Canada. Consequently, if under free trade the law of comparative advantage assigns to Canada only those industries for which the wage rates of production workers are low, then the gain from free trade in the long run—assuming that Canada could survive the short-run dislocations—would be very modest and perhaps even negative.[11]

Since advocates of free trade, such as the Wonnacotts, do not recognize the existence of high-technology industries, they interpret the consequences of free trade incorrectly and cannot comprehend what the term "industrial strategy" means. The goal of industrial strategy is to capture control of high-technology industries, which offer attractive production employment where the plants are located and attractive managerial and professional employment where the plants are controlled.

Fortunately, there has been some work on the Canadian manufacturing sector that is free of the limitations of the Wonnacotts' study. A comparative study of manufacturing industries in the U.S. and Canada by Fowler[12] is based on a realistic measure of performance. Safarian[13] collected a great deal of information on how multinational corporations operate in Canada through a comprehensive questionnaire and through interviews. Of particular note are several studies published by the Science Council of Canada on the low level of R&D in Canada, and on the causes and implications of this low level for the manufacturing sector.[14] A brief but comprehensive review of the literature on the Canadian manufacturing sector may be found in Wilkinson,[15] and Shepherd has provided an imaginative and incisive agenda for the development of an industrial strategy.[16]

Selection of the Drug Industry

The drug industry was selected for our study of the consequences for Canada of foreign ownership in the manufacturing sector for three reasons: its extremely high level of foreign ownership, its high-technology characteristics, and, most importantly, its relatively homogeneous product line. Although a number of manufacturing industries in Canada satisfy the first two conditions, few of these *also* satisfy the third condition. The drug industry is considered homogeneous because drug firms engage relatively little in the manufacture of non-drug products, and because only a very small share of the industry's output is produced by firms outside the drug industry (that is, by firms engaged primarily in the manufacture of other products and classified in other industries). This homogeneity of the drug industry contributes materially to the accuracy of the available government statistics, and, thereby, greatly increases the data's usefulness to our study.

The high level of foreign ownership in the Canadian drug industry is apparent in these 1969 statistics:

- Drug firms that were owned anywhere abroad accounted for 81.9 per cent of employee compensation, 85.9 per cent of the sales, and 87.5 per cent of the value added.
- Corresponding statistics for drug firms with U.S. parents were 68.8 per cent, 72.5 per cent and 74.5 per cent, respectively.[17]

As for high technology, the term is generally used to describe an industry in which expenditures on R&D are a large fraction of sales, and in which product innovation takes place at a high rate. Such industries commonly offer attractive employment opportunities in production. It is also true that production costs are a small fraction of the value of output, and the level of employment in production is thereby limited. However, the large gross-profit margins are mostly absorbed by the costs of managerial and professional employment—both directly and through the business services that are purchased. The drug industry satisfies all these characteristics of high technology.

There has been considerable interest in the Canadian drug industry for reasons other than the consequences of foreign ownership—an interest principally in the reasonableness of the prices paid by consumers for drug products and in the optimality of regulatory policies on the introduction of new drugs. It should be emphasized that these considerations did not enter into our decision to select the drug industry—our study is not addressed to these questions. However, investigations during the Fifties and Sixties in Canada, the U.S. and elsewhere into the prices and profits of the drug industry resulted in Canadian legislation that was designed to increase price competition. These measures and their consequences will not be ignored when we come to the consideration of alternative policies that may be adopted for the industry.

Summary and Recommendations

The following chapter, chapter 2, begins with a review of the developments prior to the Second World War that laid the foundation for the present structure of the worldwide pharmaceutical industry in the nonsocialist world. Outstanding among these developments were:

- a number of important scientific breakthroughs over the prior century that made possible the discovery of a multitude of new drugs with miraculous therapeutic value;
- changes in the patent law that allowed the patenting not only of a new drug but also variations on it;
- transfer to the physician from the pharmacist or consumer of the decision as to which manufacturer's product should be dispensed;
- government regulations on the testing of new drugs designed to ensure their safety and therapeutic benefits.

In the above environment a firm could survive and grow only if it satisfied two conditions: (1) a large R&D organization to discover, test and develop new drugs; and (2) an even larger marketing organization to realize the full profit potential of these new drugs. It was found that no national market could recover all the costs of discovering and promoting a new drug, and the need to capture each drug's worldwide profit potential forced the industry to become truly multinational. Worldwide, the industry is now dominated by about 30 giant multinational corporations, and it has about 120 smaller corporations that transcend national boundaries to varying degrees.

The industry may presently be characterized as one in which the firms are able to develop, produce and sell beneficial new drugs only by charging prices that are very high in relation to production costs. Their high gross-profit margins are made possible by R&D and marketing organizations that establish the uniqueness of each firm's products, but these margins are largely absorbed by the R&D and marketing costs that are required to maintain them. The technology involved in drug production is not trivial, but it is secondary to the R&D and marketing needed to maintain a firm's monopoly position.

Chapter 3 compares the price and expenditure performance of the Canadian and American pharmaceutical industries in 1968—the year preceding adoption in Canada of measures designed to reduce drug prices by increasing competition. To compare drug prices in the two countries, we developed comprehensive and, we believe, most accurate price indices. We found that although 1968 Canadian drug prices may have been high in relation to production costs, they were about the same as, or even slightly lower than, U.S. prices.

However, striking differences did appear in the expenditure performances of the two countries. With regard to production expenditures, a significantly higher fraction of the Canadian drug market was satisfied by imports of finished products and basic raw materials. The manufacturing activity carried on in Canada was mostly confined to secondary manufacturing, the skill content of the employment was much lower than in the U.S., and the production was dispersed over a large number of small plants that were very inefficient in their use of materials and labour.

Even more striking differences in the 1968 expenditure performances of the two countries appeared in certain of their overhead costs, which in total exceeded direct production costs. *R&D expenditures* as a percentage of sales in Canada were less than half the U.S. level. Furthermore, when the firms that were Canadian-owned (either at the time or previously) are ignored, we see that R&D expenditures in Canada approached zero: that is, the subsidiaries established here by the multinational corporations confined their R&D expenditures to the testing required to secure adoption in Canada of drugs originally introduced elsewhere. In contrast, *selling expenditures* in Canada were a much larger percentage of sales than in the U.S. The *remaining overhead costs* (apart from pretax profits) were about the same in the two countries, in spite of the much more limited scope and the lower level of management responsibilities in Canada, which should have lowered expenditures here considerably. The offsetting fact appears to be an inefficient use of a large number of low-level employees dispersed over a large number of small establishments. Finally, *pretax profits* in Canada were less than a third of their U.S. level. The difference was due both to higher production and selling costs in Canada and to the use of transfer pricing to reduce the profit figure reported to the government. Consequently, when income tax revenues were expressed as a percentage of drug sales, Canadian revenues were less than one-third U.S. revenues.

Chapter 4 repeats for 1976 the comparative analyses of chapter 3 in order to determine the influence of the measures adopted by the federal and some provincial governments in 1969 and shortly thereafter to reduce drug prices by stimulating generic competition. The legislation required compulsory licensing of patented products and authorized product selection by the pharmacist. Our comparative price indices for 1976 reveal that relative to American prices, Canadian prices for the small number of high-volume drugs for which there was generic competition fell sharply, but prices for other drugs rose enough to make the *overall* Canadian prices only slightly lower, comparatively speaking, than they were in 1968.

However, the expenditure performance of the Canadian industry is seen to have deteriorated between 1968 and 1976 relative to that in the U.S. The fraction of sales satisfied by imports actually *rose*, and production in Canada declined, with no evidence that it became more efficient. R&D expenditures as a fraction of sales rose in the U.S., but not in Canada; the sharp rise in the general level of employee compensation rates in Canada suggests that the real quantity of R&D actually fell here. Selling expenditures were reduced in response to the government's competition policy and to previous criticism of their high levels. Other overhead costs remained about the same percentage of sales in the face of the sharp rise in Canadian compensation rates, either because overhead activities were rationalized or because the activities were further centralized in head offices abroad.

The generally accepted image of the multinational corporation is that it transfers production and other activities to a host country as sales increase with the passage of time. However, this process was actually reversed in Canada between 1968 and 1976, either because the multinationals were responding to the competition policy that they opposed very bitterly, or because production was being transferred to Puerto Rico, Ireland and other countries that offered lower wage rates and exemption from income taxes. Even the home countries of the multinationals lost production and reported profits.

Finally, chapter 5 examines various policy options for improving the industry's performance. That objective can be sought either through policies that are concerned directly with *performance* (but without explicit concern for the foreign-ownership consequences), or through explicit concern for the foreign-ownership consequences), or through

14

policies that are designed to increase Canadian *ownership* in the hope of improving performance.

Among the policy options that are directly concerned with performance, we conclude that the continuation of present policies is very unattractive. The government's competition policy will diminish in effectiveness with the passage of time, because the industry is developing countervailing strategies. Furthermore, under present policies the substitution of imports for domestic production will continue at an accelerated rate, and R&D here will continue to stagnate. The alternatives to present government policies are either less or more interventionist. The drug industry would, of course, like to see less interventionist policies, in particular the abandonment of compulsory licensing. The industry would probably respond with some increase in R&D in Canada, since we already have some natural advantages for locating R&D here. We favour more interventionist policies and propose some that are quite consistent with the existing framework of government/business relations. We show that they could materially improve the performance of the industry—both by reducing prices to consumers and by increasing R&D in Canada. Arresting the substitution of imports for domestic production is possible, but reversing it is found to be a more difficult and questionable goal.

Our examination of the various ways in which Canadian ownership in the drug industry could be increased makes clear that maintaining the degree that existed prior to the Second World War would have been far less difficult and expensive than restoring it would be today. Here, as elsewhere, an ounce of prevention would have been worth at least a pound of cure. Now, aggressive policies to reduce drastically foreign ownership in the drug industry would involve great costs and provide only modest benefits. It is our judgment that a cost-benefit analysis would give a much higher priority to increasing domestic ownership in a number of other industries than in the drug industry.

However, the performance policies discussed earlier will contribute in the *long run* to an increased domestic ownership of the Canadian drug industry, just as will policies that are concerned directly with that goal. Our review of the Canada Development Corporation and its involvement in the "life sciences" industry reveals that CDC has maintained and expanded Connaught Laboratories, the only important Canadian firm in the drug industry. More important, CDC is providng a substantial financial and technical foundation—the only such foundation—for Canadian participation in the exciting new field of genetic engineering.

The general conclusion one may draw from this study is that in a worldwide economy dominated by multinational corporations, the welfare of a country cannot be left to the so-called free play of market forces. The worldwide activities of a multinational corporation are carried on to achieve *its* long-run growth and stability—with little consideration for the overall economic welfare of the various countries in which it operates. In particular, it formulates and implements plans to sell its products in *all* markets, and its production, R&D and other activities in each country are determined by applying its strategic and tactical goals to its worldwide opportunities. Consequently, the alternatives for Canada are either passive stagnation or the judicious use of ownership, expenditure and competition policies to advance the national welfare.

Historical Perspectives on the Drug Industry

2

The mid-Thirties were a watershed in the history of the pharmaceutical industry. It has been said that "a pneumonia patient, given a reasonable environment and nursing care, probably stood almost as good a chance of recovery in the days of Galen [c. 130-200 A.D.] as he did in 1935."[1] That was, of course, before the advent of the antibiotics that were to transform the industry. The basic scientific discoveries that led to the development of antibiotics all predate this period, but the genesis of the modern pharmaceutical industry can be seen to be Dr. Domagk's discovery in 1935 of the bactericidal properties of Prontosil, a red dye derived from coal tar.[2]

Early History

Very little progress was made in the development of new drugs in the fifteen centuries between 200 and 1700 A.D. Less than two dozen effective drugs were known before the year 1700, and almost all were of natural origin—of animal, vegetable or mineral extraction. Folk remedies abounded. The few effective drugs that existed were prescribed along with many other products that frequently were either useless or dangerous. Indicative of the state of development is the fact that the pharmaceutical industry (if it could be so called) in England during the Middle Ages was in the hands of the "spicers," who dealt in both medicinal and culinary products. The eighteenth century saw a number of important advances, including smallpox vaccination, treatment for scurvy with citrus fruits, and the study of the action of digitalis on the heart. The first not only contributed significantly to improved health standards and life expectancy but also laid the groundwork for the development of other vaccines in the nineteenth century. The second provided the initial insights into the function of vitamins in the diet. The third was among the first complete

17

observations of the effect of drugs on the human body that set the standard for future clinical examination.

During the nineteenth century discoveries were made on three separate fronts that laid the foundation for the modern industry. First was the extraction of the active principles from materials of natural origin, particularly the alkaloids, such as morphine from opium, caffeine from tea and coffee, and quinine from cinchona bark. For the first time these drugs were available in pure form so that their therapeutic properties (beneficial and adverse) could be studied under controlled conditions. The need for high standards of quality and purity began to be recognized. Parallel to this was the realization that brand new chemicals synthesized in the laboratory also might have therapeutic effects. Ether was shown in 1846 to have anaesthetic properties, leading to the development of other anaesthetics. Coal tar derivatives had recently come into existence, along with a wide variety of new products (particularly dyestuffs) whose therapeutic properties could be studied. In 1860 salicylic acid (from which aspirin was to be developed subsequently) was synthesized, the first drug to be a by-product of the research on dyes. Phenacetin and antipyrine were by-products of coal tar chemistry. Bacteriology was the third front along which discoveries were being made. Pasteur showed that there was a causal link between bacteria and disease. This led him to the development of vaccines against anthrax and rabies. The nineteenth century produced an increase in the understanding of disease, better diagnosis of disease, and improvements in public health, but it brought no great increase in either the number or types of drugs available to the physician. The majority of drugs in use by 1900 were still limited primarily to purgatives, emetics and narcotics.

The twentieth century saw significant advances in the development of drugs, both from traditional sources and from laboratory synthesis. Along traditional lines, a major breakthrough in the first quarter of the century was the discovery by Banting and Best in Toronto in 1922 that insulin extracted from animal pancreatic tissue would alleviate the effects of diabetes. The mass production and distribution of insulin, however, presented a number of significant problems that till then had not been faced. The solution of those problems was to stand the industry in good stead when subsequently it was called upon to mass produce and deliver antibiotics in the Forties.

In the realm of synthetic drug development, Paul Ehrlich can be regarded as the founder of modern chemotherapy. Building on Koch's observation that bacteria could be selectively stained by certain dyestuffs, he hypothesized that if chemicals could be synthesized that would selectively attach themselves to and kill disease bacteria without harming healthy tissue, then it should be possible to design drugs to be taken internally that would destroy disease bacteria without harming the patient. This hypothesis was confirmed by his discoveries of atoxyl to treat sleeping sickness and arsphenamine to treat syphilis. Not until Domagk's experiments using Prontosil to cure streptococcal infections in 1935, however, were any further discoveries made along these lines. The active ingredient in Prontosil was soon found to be sulphanilamide, and attempts to improve its efficacy spawned the development of related and better products. The discovery of penicillin in 1928 and its availability in therapeutically useful quantities in 1940 broadened the range of antibiotics. Chemotherapy was well on its way. The traditional role of the pharmacist was transferred to the chemist, pharmacologist and clinician.

One result of these discoveries and advances made in chemical analysis and synthesis had been a change in the source of drugs. Naturally occurring substances (now referred to as biologicals) may contain—despite careful preparation by sophisticated methods and intense quality control—traces of extraneous material, or they may not duplicate the human material. For example, animal insulin is not identical to human insulin, and a small fraction of diabetics cannot tolerate the former. When a natural material has been found to exhibit therapeutic effects, the first step is to try to isolate its active ingredient, primarily to control the effect of the drug on the patient by eliminating unnecessary impurities, but also to analyze its structure and ultimately to synthesize and improve it. Once the chemical structure is known and synthesis is accomplished, it is frequently possible to modify the structure so as to increase the beneficial effects and/or reduce the adverse ones. (Examples are sulpha drugs that act against a wider range of bacterial infections with fewer side reactions than did the original sulphanilamide.) Sometimes this leads to drugs with entirely new therapeutic effects, and it has been stated, ''Today changing the molecules of drugs of known effectiveness is the most common method of looking for new drugs.''[3] The spectacular payoff to research along these lines has resulted in the pharmaceutical industry investing heavily in research.

The dyestuff industry was the precursor of the modern drug industry. Germany quickly became the leader in dyestuff research and production. In the middle of the nineteenth century, the dyestuff industry was intensely competitive in an innovative sense. The

19

industry was dependent on the textile industry for the bulk of its sales, and the latter was, in turn, subject to the whims and vagaries of fashion. The textile manufacturers, therefore, maintained a steady pressure on the dyestuff producers for new products to keep pace with changing styles, making the level of innovation and product obsolescence high. The key to success was research, rather than elaborate and efficient production facilities. The required ingredient was a trained and motivated supply of chemists, which was readily available from German and Swiss universities. Consequently, the dyestuff industry flourished in both Germany and Switzerland, where both dyes and drugs were in those days synthesized from coal tar. It was a short step from dye to drug discovery and production, and these two countries were to remain dominant in the drug industry until the First World War.

Development of the U.S. Industry

The U.S. drug industry started at the time of the War of American Independence, when the new nation had to make its own drugs or go without. A number of indigenous drug firms were established during the late eighteenth and early nineteenth centuries. These companies restricted their activities to extracting natural products from indigenous sources or to importing natural extracts from abroad and compounding them locally. Innovation was restricted to improving the methods of "making tablets, extracts and mixtures more stable and palatable."[4] Early in the twentieth century the U.S. market had become sufficiently significant that several European drug firms established subsidiaries in the U.S. to market their imported products.

The First World War found the U.S. almost entirely dependent on Germany for supplies of synthetic drugs, since the latter dominated worldwide production and the concomitant technology. Again it was a question of "make your own or do without." The U.S. industry took up the challenge and was able to duplicate the synthetic drugs that had hitherto been imported. This experience fostered the expansion of U.S. research and production, particularly in vitamins, hormones, serums and vaccines—many of which were natural products or based on fermentation processes. Between the two world wars the German industry re-established its U.S. subsidiaries but was not able to displace the now entrenched domestic industry. The successful commercialization of insulin had contributed to both the self-confidence and the reputation of the U.S. industry and provided it with the skills to repeat the process when necessary. The Second World War again provided a strong impetus for drug production and research in the U.S. by increasing demand and cutting off supplies from Europe. Despite the original sulpha drug being discovered in Germany, the active ingredient being isolated in France, and the first broadly acting commercial drug being developed in the U.K., the U.S. industry rapidly developed its own analogues and was soon the world leader in sulpha production.

The new technology significantly changed the character of the industry, but other factors also contributed to its evolution. Pre-eminent among these other factors were the impact of regulation and the application of the patent laws to the newly discovered drugs. Government regulation of drugs in the U.S. goes back to the 1906 Pure Food and Drug Act.[5] The primary purpose of this act was to prevent and control the adulteration of food. Drug regulation was secondary and was aimed at protecting the public from medical quacks and at prohibiting the sale of dangerous substances. The advent of the sulfa drugs and the Elixci Sulfanilamide tragedy of 1937 (in which a toxic solvent was used as a carrier for a sulfa drug, resulting in over a hundred deaths) provided an impetus to tighten the regulations. It was evident that there were significant risks associated with the introduction of new drugs and, therefore, a need for safety tests to ensure that toxic products would not be sold to an unsuspecting public.

The 1938 Food, Drug and Cosmetic Act concentrated on these safety aspects, describing procedures for the premarketing clearance of new drugs, and requiring increased information on the drug label. The regulations interpreting the act created a distinction between over-the-counter drugs and prescription drugs. The former, which bore detailed labels describing the product and giving the recommended dosage, could be purchased by anyone at will. The latter had limited labeling information and could only be purchased with a doctor's prescription. Prior to 1938 there had been both prescription and over-the-counter sales, but generally any nonnarcotic drug could be purchased without a prescription. As a result, drug companies did not direct their advertising toward doctors through the medical literature, preferring instead to address the ultimate consumer directly through the popular press. The 1938 act effectively changed the way in which prescription drugs were marketed. The decision as to whether a drug would be sold by prescription or over the counter was left entirely to the discretion of the drug companies. Most new drugs introduced after 1938 were designated as prescription drugs. As a consequence, the purchasing decision was shifted from the patient to the doctor, and the doctor—as decision maker—became the customer, making it more effective to direct the marketing of drugs toward the medical profession than toward the actual consumer. Given the emergency circumstances under which drugs are usually purchased, it is reasonable to expect that their demand is relatively price inelastic, that is, the quantity purchased is insensitive to the price. Under the new regulations, the doctor, as customer, prescribes but does not pay for the drugs, and probably does not even know their prices. The net effect is to increase the price inelasticity even further.[6]

The interpretation of patent law also had its effect on the industry. It was ruled that the original antibiotics (sulfanilamide and penicillin) could not be patented: the former, because it was a previously known material; and the latter, because it was naturally occurring and because the U.S. government had been crucially involved in its early development. As a result, penicillin became a highly competitive product. Between 1944 and 1950 the share of the five largest penicillin producers fell from 88 per cent to 43 per cent of total sales, and between 1945 and 1950 the price of penicillin fell from $4,495 to $282 per pound. Had this same situation applied to other antibiotics, the development of the U.S. pharmaceutical industry might have been very different.

The landmark decision was the 1948 ruling on the Waksman patent application for protection of the technique that was used to discover streptomycin. Although streptomycin is a naturally occurring substance and, therefore, on the face of it, not patentable, the ruling held that the chemical modifications required to enable it to be purified created a new product and a new process, both of which were patentable. As a result, Merck, a major pharmaceutical company, obtained a very strong patent position (a composition-of-matter patent). The Waksman patent stimulated R&D in two ways. First, the search for fundamentally new drugs was stimulated by the fact that now a company could obtain patent protection on specific drugs and specific processes. Secondly, the chemical modification of a patented drug by "molecular manipulation" could produce a "new" drug with the same or possibly improved properties, but the modification would fall outside the competitor's patent protection and might even be patentable in its own right. As a result, the U.S. drug industry has become highly competitive at the research and marketing levels rather than at the product level.

The final evolutionary link in the industry's structural chain was provided when the companies decided to exploit the patents themselves (rather than license other producers) and to control the marketing of their products by forward integration. A company achieved the latter by establishing its own sales force ("detail men") to call directly on the physicians, rather than relying on wholesalers and other distributors to "sell" its products. Temin argues that each new product is initially sold at a monopoly price in order to secure extraordinary profits for the innovating firm, but the same result could be achieved if the technology were licensed at a sufficiently high royalty rate. He estimated that the royalty rate would have to be very much higher than the 2.5 to 4 per cent of sales then prevailing in the industry. At the very least, a royalty of 40 to 50 per cent of sales would be necessary, but that would be seen as predatory, while exploitation through monopoly pricing disguises the situation for a time.

The historical developments described above had a decisive influence on how competition evolved in the industry. Price competition is extremely destructive when demand is price inelastic, but the industry avoided destructive price wars by following the classic pattern of monopolistic competition. Large-scale marketing expenditures were undertaken to make product differentiation—not price—the channel of competition. Through the use of patents, trademarks, advertising and intensive "detailing" to physicians, the prices of the wonder drugs were kept stable throughout the Fifties at levels far above their production costs, despite other producers entering the market for each type of drug. Although molecular manipulation, which allowed firms to develop close substitutes for newly patented drugs rather quickly, could have resulted in vigorous price competition, it was not allowed to do so.

By the late Fifties the now familiar criticisms of the industry had started to gather force—criticisms that its advertising is excessive and misleading, its selling costs are unnecessarily high, and its research and development is directed toward simple substitutes for competitors' products rather than toward genuine scientific advances. Competition between firms did—and does—exist, acting to reduce monopoly profits, but such competition is mainly based on research and marketing expenditures to differentiate a product—it is not price competition. It should be pointed out in the industry's defence, however, that the nonprice competition has resulted in some price attrition over time and has increased the number of new products available on the market. And even though many of these new drugs may only be imitations of existing products, some genuine advances have nonetheless been made.[7]

There is no doubt that the industry developed along oligopolistic lines. Apologists for the industry, however, point to the fact that by normal measurement standards it is not a highly concentrated industry, since the four and the eight largest firms in 1972 had only 25 and 43 per cent of total sales, respectively.[8] Unfortunately, though, the reported concentration data are deficient in that they are based on production rather than on the market. There is considerable

TABLE 2-1

PERCENTAGES OF TOTAL ETHICAL DRUG SALES IN CERTAIN THERAPEUTIC CLASSES, FOR SELECTED PHARMACEUTICAL COMPANIES, 1973

Company	Therapeutic Class	Per Cent of Sales
Astra	Anaesthetics	19.7
	Cardiovasculars	14.0
	Antibiotics	10.3
	Total	44.0
Eli Lilly	Antibiotics	57.4
	Analgesics	14.7
	Total	72.1
Syntex	Dermatologicals	46.3
	Reproductive agents	31.6
	Total	77.9
Upjohn	Antibiotics	27.0
	Hormones	17.7
	Antidiabetics	7.2
	Total	51.9

Source: Barrie G. James, *The Future of the Pharmaceutical Industry to 1990* (London: Associated Business Programmes, 1977), p. 36.

homogeneity in the research and production processes and in the chemical entities used within the industry, but the end products serve a wide variety of different medical markets. Products can be classified by various therapeutic classes, depending on the different bodily

TABLE 2-2
DOMINATION OF SELECTED THERAPEUTIC CLASSES, BY MAJOR PHARMACEUTICAL COMPANIES, 1973

Therapeutic Class	Pharmaceutical Companies
Analgesics	Bayer, Sterling Drug, Lilly
Anthelmintics	Bayer, Sterling Drug, Warner-Lambert
Antibiotics	Beecham, Bristol-Meyers, Lederle, Lilly, Pfizer
Cardiovascular agents	Boehringer Ingelheim, Ciba-Geigy, Hoechst, ICI, Johnson and Johnson, Merck, Sandoz-Wander
Dermatologicals	Ciba-Geigy, Glaxo, Schering AG, Schering-Plough, Syntex
Hormones	Lederle, Merck, Roussel, Searle, Schering AG, Schering-Plough, Syntex, Upjohn
Nonsteroidal anti-inflammatory agents	Boots/Upjohn, Ciba-Geigy, Merck, Syntex
Oral contraceptives	Akzo, Johnson and Johnson, Schering AG, Searle, Syntex, Warner-Lambert
Psychotherapeutics	American Home, Johnson and Johnson, Merck, Pfizer, Hoffmann–La Roche
Respiratory agents	Boehringer Ingelheim, Fisons, Glaxo
Vitamins	Merck, Hoffmann–La Roche, U.S. Vitamin

Source: Barrie G. James, *The Future of the Pharmaceutical Industry to 1990* (London: Associated Business Programmes, 1977), p. 37.

25

TABLE 2-3

IMPORTANT NEW DRUGS INTRODUCED IN THE UNITED STATES, BY THERAPEUTIC CLASS AND MARKETING COMPANIES, 1959-68

Year	Drug	Therapeutic Class	Marketing Companies
1959	Griseofulvin	Antibiotic	Schering, McNeil, Ayerst
	Phenformin	Antidiabetic	U.S. Vitamin
	Thiotepa	Antineoplastic	Lederle
	Imipramine	Antidepressant	Geigy
1960	Methicillin	Antibiotic	Bristol
	Guanethidine	Antihypertensive	Ciba
	Glucagon	Blood-sugar regulator	Lilly
	Spironolactone	Diuretic	Searle
1961	Cyclophosphamide	Antineoplastic	Mead Johnson
	Vinblastine	Antineoplastic	Lilly
	Live poliomyelitis vaccine	Vaccine	Several
1962	Fluorouracil	Antineoplastic	Roche
1963	Methyldopa	Antihypertensive	Merck Sharp & Dohme
	Measles vaccines	Vaccine	Several
	Penicillamine	Copper-binding agent	Merck Sharp & Dohme
1964	Ampicillin	Antibiotic	Ayerst, Bristol
	Dactinomycin	Antineoplastic	Merck Sharp & Dohme
	Cephalothin	Antibiotic	Lilly

Year	Drug	Therapeutic Class	Marketing Companies
1965	Lincomycin	Antibiotic	Upjohn
	Indomethacin	Analgesic and anti-inflammatory drug	Merck Sharp & Dohme
1966	Bentamicin	Antibiotic	Schering
	Allopurinol	Antigout drug	Burroughs Wellcome
	Furosemide	Diuretic	Hoechst
	Amantadine	Antiviral drug	Dupont
1967	Clofibrate	Drug used to reduce blood cholesterol	Ayerst
	Clomiphene	Antisterility drug	Merrell
	Ethacrynic acid	Diuretic	Merck Sharp & Dohme
	Ethambutol	Antituberculous drug	Lederle
	Pentaxocine	Analgesic	Winthrop
1968	Propanolol	Anti-arrhythmia drug	Ayerst
	Azathioprine	Inhibitor of the immunologic response	Burroughs Wellcome
	Desferoxamine mesylate	Iron-binding agent	Ciba
	Anti-Ph antibody	Drug used to prevent formation by mother of anti-bodies to Rh-positive infant	Ortho

Source: Harry F. Dowling, *Medicines for Man* (New York: Alfred A. Knopf, 1970), p. 99.

functions or types of diseases they deal with, and each firm tends to concentrate its efforts in only a few therapeutic classes. Thus, although there may be a few hundred firms in the industry, there are relatively few firms competing in each therapeutic class. Tables 2-1 to 2-3 give some typical evidence of this.

Multinational Character of the Industry

Developments similar to those described above for the U.S. industry took place in other countries, and they explain the multinational character of the industry that evolved. The short life cycle of a product that results from competition in research and marketing and from limited patent protection compels the producer to extract monopoly rents simultaneously from as many markets as possible. It has been stated that "no therapeutic group in any national market offers the volume of sales necessary to recover current development and marketing costs and produce an adequate return on investment."[9] The necessity and ability to transport across national borders not only a firm's patented product but also its marketing practices, allowed the establishment of a strong brand image and the extraction of monopoly rents in many markets.

The incentive to develop multinationally was further enhanced by the technology of production, which for ethical drugs is a two-stage process: chemical synthesis, and then the compounding of these chemicals into pharmaceutical preparations. The pharmaceutical chemicals (or fine chemicals as they are also known) are the active ingredients of the ethical drugs. The production of fine chemicals usually requires multistage synthesis over long periods, with heavy costs for maintaining quality control over raw materials and finished product. Economies of scale are to be found in this stage of the production process. Consequently, the production of fine chemicals takes place almost exclusively within only one or a few of the production facilities of a large multinational firm. For example, Hoffmann–La Roche employs only two plants to produce its worldwide requirements of carotenoids (vitamin A precursors).[10]

The production of pharmaceutical preparations involves converting chemicals into the familiar form dispensed by the pharmacist. For this to be done, they are combined with other chemicals, fillers, flavours, sweeteners and coatings, and they are then pelletized in dosage form and packaged. The principal requirements at this stage are cleanliness and strict quality control. The technology is modest compared with that required for fine chemicals. This compounding stage can easily be divorced from the fine chemical stage, since they have no direct link and there are no significant economies of scale to be exploited. Typically, then, a multinational will centralize its fine chemical production while establishing final-dosage manufacturing plants around the world, so as to be seen as a producer in each local market and to take advantage of tariff protection wherever possible.

Research and development is the key element in a firm's technology. It is usually located, therefore, close to corporate headquarters. On the other hand, fine chemical production can be located at any hospitable place in the world.[11] Although it requires highly technical skills, these are, nevertheless, relatively routine (production, engineering, and quality control), and the product has a high value-to-weight ratio. Furthermore, these chemicals are not marketed by the producers in an intermediate form, allowing, therefore, the establishment of arbitrary transfer prices between affiliates in order to recognize profits in low-tax countries. Hence, it is not the least bit surprising that the industry has developed a strong multinational character, given these incentives.

The essential features of the multinational drug industry may now be characterized as follows. If a firm's products have no patent protection or brand-name identification, the firm can only compete with price, and its operation will be marginal with no long-run prospects for growth or even survival. To have a secure position in the industry requires large R&D expenditures, both to develop new products and to carry out the human testing required for government approval. Not only must these expenditures be large, they must be incurred long before any revenues can result. As in the search for oil and gas, many drug products are "dry wells" that never come to market. Others barely recover their R&D investment, and a few become highly successful. To recover the combined R&D investment on all products, the successful ones must generate very high gross profits, but that is possible only through marketing expenditures, which add to the cost. In short, we have an industry that enjoys a very high margin between price and production costs, but a large fraction of the gross profits must be expended on the R&D and marketing costs required to maintain the gross profits. While the technology of producing fine chemicals also contributes to this industry structure, it is secondary to the role of R&D and marketing.

As will be discussed in the following section, the industry has been criticized strongly by various writers and government agencies for charging exorbitant prices and reaping excessive profits. Industry supporters have countered that industry profits *on average* have not been excessive, if one recognizes that exceptional growth and high risk require a higher rate of profit than the average for industry in general. Regardless, the industry could continue functioning in its present form with some reduction in marketing expenditures and in prices. However, any large reduction in prices would require the effective elimination of the industry's marketing activities, ending the product differentiation and gross-profit margins required to support R&D. In that event, new product development would have to become the responsibility of the public sector, an alternative that many believe would be more costly and less productive.

Unfavourable Developments for the Industry

Unfortunately for the industry, it experienced in the postwar period some failures as well as many successes, and these failures along with the industry's high prices and profits have become the subject of critical government investigations in Canada, the U.S. and elsewhere. The legislation that followed, and certain other developments to be discussed below, began eroding the profitability of the industry in these countries. In the U.S., amendments to the Food, Drug and Cosmetics Act were introduced in 1962 by Senator Estes Kefauver as a result of testimony heard at the 1959 Anti-Trust and Monopoly Subcommittee hearings. At those hearings the industry was accused of promoting nonefficacious drugs at high prices as a result of the patent protection afforded the industry's products, consumer and physician ignorance, and the indifference of doctors to product price when prescribing medication. The 1962 amendments were actually triggered by the well-known thalidomide crisis and were aimed at increasing government regulation so as to improve the accuracy of information disseminated by manufacturers. The final amended act, together with the accompanying regulations, prescribed closer control over premarket testing of drugs and tighter criteria for the approval of new drugs. The effect of the amended act has been to increase vastly the cost of introducing new drugs and to lengthen the time between discovery and marketing. Defenders of the industry hold that the new legislation has also produced a noticeable disincentive to research, reducing significantly the industry's output of new drugs. It has been estimated that the cost of introducing a new drug rose ten times between the early Fifties and the late Sixties.[12] Table 2-4 certainly confirms that the number of new chemical entities introduced into the market after 1962 dropped sharply.

30

TABLE 2-4
ANNUAL APPROVALS OF NEW CHEMICAL ENTITIES (NCEs) BY THE FOOD AND DRUG ADMINISTRATION, 1950-75

Year	No. of NCEs	Year	No. of NCEs	Year	No. of NCEs
1950	44	1960	55	1970	17
51	55	61	43	71	17
52	40	62	30	72	11
53	73	63	13	73	18
54	60	64	25	74	16
55	57	65	23	75	12
56	52	66	18		
57	73	67	23		
58	45	68	7		
59	76	69	12		

Source: Henry Grabowski, *Drug Regulation and Innovation* (American Enterprise Institute, 1976), p. 18, as reprinted in W. Duncan Reekie and Michael H. Weber, *Profits, Politics and Drugs* (New York: Holmes and Meier, 1979), p.8.

The hurdles introduced by the 1962 amendments, however, are certainly not the only explanation for this decline. Current technology and drugs have been highly successful in conquering bacterial and microbial diseases. Tumours and viral diseases, however, present a different set of problems and require new technology. The latter two act within the cell—not outside as do bacteria and microbes—and require, therefore, a new understanding of cell chemistry and a new set of chemical entities.[13] Perhaps the industry has reached a technological plateau, with decreasing returns to additional research, that will continue until a new breakthrough is achieved.

The Sixties saw a reduction—most noticeably in the U.S.—in the number of new drug products introduced by the industry, together with falling profit margins and decreasing investments in R&D. It should be pointed out, however, that this reduction in new products was not accompanied by a diminution in important new therapeutic advances; they remained constant at three or four per year throughout the decade, as is indicated by the last line of Table 2-5. This implies that the 1962 amendments had their greatest effect on simple imitations and minor modifications of existing drugs. The amendments also put the cost of developing and introducing new products beyond the financial capacity of all but the largest firms, thereby limiting the entry of new firms and reducing competition.

31

TABLE 2-5
NUMBER OF NEW DRUGS MARKETED IN THE UNITED STATES, 1959-68

	1959	1960	1961	1962	1963	1964	1965	1966	1967	1968
New single chemicals	63	45	39	27	16	17	23	12	25	11
Duplicate single products	49	62	32	43	34	29	18	15	25	26
Compounded products	203	199	189	180	149	111	71	53	32	50
Total new products	315	306	260	250	199	157	112	80	82	87
New dosage forms (not included above)	104	98	106	84	52	41	22	26	14	21
New chemical entities	32	30	14	10	7	6	4	7	9	7
Important therapeutic advances	4	3	3	1	3	3	2	3	4	4

Source: Harry F. Dowling, *Medicines for Man* (New York: Alfred A. Knopf, 1970), p. 98.

Another development that may have contributed to the falling of profit margins was the gradual introduction of generic equivalents for the trademarked drugs. As a patent protection ran out, new firms would enter the market and produce drugs that were chemically equivalent to the trademarked product, but sell them under the generic (chemical) name with little promotion or advertising. Generic producers are typically marginal firms that compete with the brand-name producers on the basis of price. Their advent has contributed to lower prices, but the effect has been small, since physicians for the most part have been slow to switch from brand-name to generic prescribing for a number of reasons. First, the long and controversial debate in the profession about the relative merits and shortcomings of generic equivalents has sown doubt and uncertainty in the minds of physicians. Proponents of generic prescribing claim that these substitutes are fully equivalent to the brand-name originals. Opponents, on the other hand, cite studies that show deficiencies in the bio-availability and quality of generic products.[14] Secondly, physicians tend to be much less aware of the existence of specific generic substitutes because they are not advertised to any great extent. And finally, the major drug firms all coin simple and evocative brand names for their products, whereas the generic name is usually long, complex and difficult to remember.[15] The physician tends to prescribe what he remembers rather than the cheaper alternative.

The Industry in Canada

The development of the Canadian pharmaceutical industry has followed quite closely the pattern of other high-technology, multinational industries.[16] The general pattern has involved the establishment of a sales subsidiary to sell imported products in the Canadian market in order to satisfy local demand, and the introduction of secondary manufacturing as it becomes profitable.

As long as a foreign firm had a strong patent position, it had little incentive to establish manufacturing facilities in Canada. But once competition became established through the export to Canada of substitutes for the original brand-name product—substitutes that fell outside patent protection—the tariff could be used to strengthen the original firm's position. The tariff on chemical products (including pharmaceutical) is such that imported products similar to a "class or kind made in Canada" carry a higher tariff than imported products of a kind not made in Canada. For many years the Department of National

Revenue chose to interpret the definition of a "class or kind made in Canada" as broadly as possible so as to include any substitute for a domestically made product. A ruling that a product is made in Canada could be obtained if the finished product was made in Canadian facilities with about 20 to 25 per cent of its value being added in Canada. Such a ruling was almost tailor-made for the pharmaceutical industry, because the basic chemicals could be imported, the compounding operations could be carried out locally, and the value-added requirement could be met. The tariff on the imported substitute would increase from 15 to 20 per cent, while the basic chemicals, which represented a small fraction of the cost for the product made in Canada, would continue to pay only 15 per cent duty or come in duty-free. Consequently, other foreign firms would have to establish manufacturing facilities in Canada to offset the original firm's competitive advantage.

Once production facilities had been established in Canada, the size of the Canadian operation would grow with sales and with the introduction of additional products. However, the subsidiary would remain a "truncated branch-plant" operation, engaged in secondary manufacturing and sales, since there was no incentive for backward integration into the manufacture of fine chemicals,[17] or for undertaking R&D, or for undertaking other activities that could be confined to headquarters.

Canada's first pharmaceutical operation was founded in Toronto in 1879 by E.B. Shuttleworth.[18] In 1887 it was followed by the establishment in Windsor of a subsidiary (the first in Canada) by Parke Davis and Company. Among other well-known companies establishing sales offices in Canada before the First World War were: Wyeth (1883), Allen and Hanbury's (1902), Burroughs Wellcome (1906), Lederle Laboratories (1910), and Sharp and Dohme (1911). Charles E. Frosst and Company was founded in 1899 and became one of the most important domestic drug firms. The period between the wars saw the establishment of sales offices in Canada by many of the other traditionally well-known multinationals in the industry, such as Abbott Laboratories, Eli Lilly, Hoffmann-La Roche, Ciba, Rhone Poulenc, Sandoz, Squibb, and Upjohn, to name a few. All of these expanded beyond selling operations into limited manufacture and, in some instances, into limited R&D. A number of domestic firms, including Ayerst, McKenna and Harrison, Connaught Laboratories, and Mowatt and Moore, were started during this period.

Prior to the therapeutic revolution and the transformation of the industry described earlier, the research and the marketing requirements for a successful position in the Canadian pharmaceutical industry were quite modest, and domestic firms were able to thrive side by side with their foreign-based competitors. Later, though, their acquisition by a foreign multinational became imperative—or at least highly profitable—for both parties. For instance, Ayerst responded to the therapeutic revolution by establishing before the Second World War a large and vigorous R&D organization that proved to be quite successful in terms of product discovery. However, the Canadian market was not large enough to generate the gross profits needed to support the continued operation of this R&D activity. The testing, marketing and other activities required for Ayerst to invade foreign markets would require further investment that was large and risky in relation to the firm's size. At the same time, Ayerst's soon-to-be parent company, American Home Products, had the resources and expertise needed for entry into the U.S. and other markets, and it was interested in further diversification in the pharmaceutical field. Consequently, the large difference between the value of Ayerst as an independent company and its value as a subsidiary of American Home Products made the latter's acquisition of Ayerst mutually profitable. In fact, Ayerst's ability to survive as an independent company was even open to question.

Ayerst was acquired by American Home Products in 1943. To mention a few of the other acquisitions that took place: E.B. Shuttleworth Chemical Company was bought by Pitman-Moore in 1957; Frank W. Horner, by Carter Products in 1963; and Charles E. Frosst, by Merck, Sharp and Dohme in 1965. In addition, the postwar period saw the establishment of many other foreign firms in Canada, such as Geigy, Fisons, Hoechst, and William S. Merrell. Whereas the domestically owned share of the industry had been quite significant prior to the Second World War, the postwar wave of acquisitions left only one domestically owned firm of any significance, Connaught Laboratories, which was owned by the University of Toronto—not by persons in the private sector.[19] The other surviving Canadian-owned firms were very small and had either found a small niche in a very narrow market or had specialized in the manufacture of generic equivalents that could compete with brand-name products on the basis of price.

TABLE 2-6
COMPARISON OF PHARMACEUTICAL ESTABLISHMENTS
OPERATING IN CANADA UNDER FOREIGN AND DOMESTIC
CONTROL, 1969
(%)

	Under Foreign Control			Under Domestic Control
	U.S.	European	Total	
Number of establishments	34.7	8.0	42.7	57.3
Number of production workers	61.2	10.5	71.7	28.3
Total production wages	63.5	10.8	74.3	25.7
Number of nonproduction employees	69.9	14.1	84.0	16.0
Total salaries	71.2	14.1	85.3	14.7
Total employees	66.2	12.6	78.8	21.2
Total remuneration	68.8	13.1	81.9	18.7
Shipment of goods of own manufacture	72.5	13.5	85.9	14.1
Value added from manufacturing	74.5	13.1	87.5	12.5

Source: Statistics Canada, *Domestic and Foreign Control of Manufacturing Establishments in Canada, 1969 and 1970* (Ottawa: 1976), p. 64.

Table 2-6 clearly shows the state of the Canadian-controlled sector of the industry in 1969. Although 57.3 per cent of the establishments were Canadian controlled, they only made 14.1 per cent of the shipments of goods of own manufacture and only accounted for 12.5 per cent of the value added from manufacturing. Further evidence of the relative underdevelopment of the Canadian industry is given in the report of the U.K. Banks Committee:

> that 85 per cent of drug manufacture in Canada was confined to the conversion of imported material into final-dosage form, that at least 95 per cent of Canadian drug patents were owned by residents of foreign countries, and that expenditure on pharmaceutical research in Canada was at a comparatively low level.[20]

It may be added that the market structure of the industry in Canada is similar to that in the United States. In 1968 the four and the eight largest Canadian firms had 26.1 and 40.0 per cent of total sales, respectively,[21] percentages that are similar to the U.S. figures quoted earlier. Given the manner in which firms in the industry specialize in different therapeutic markets, however, these concentration figures are not a true measure of the degree of competition in the Canadian industry.

The relationship between the industry and the Canadian government has not been a smooth one, particularly for the dominant foreign-owned sector. For the better part of a decade the industry was under investigation or scrutiny. The process started in April 1958 (prior to the Kefauver Commission) with an inquiry (under Section 42 of the Combines Investigation Act) by the director of investigation and research of the Restrictive Trade Practices Commission (RTPC). His initial report was submitted in February 1961 and led to a series of public hearings and a final RTPC report in January 1963. The conclusions drawn in both of these reports have an important bearing on the legislation that followed several years later. The director in his report stated:

> The dominance of branches and subsidiaries of United States drug firms and the widespread use in Canada of drug products originated in the United States mean that the drug trade in Canada in effect operates under the United States patent system. Products are patented in the United States and their prices set on the basis that the patent holders have a legal monopoly on the sale of these products. Corresponding Canadian patents are then obtained and the drug is supplied to the Canadian market . . . at at least as high a price as that charged in the United States.[22]

Although Canadian patent legislation has for some time provided for compulsory licensing of food and drug products, the RTPC report found that Canadian firms were not generally availing themselves of this right. The monopolistic nature of the industry was maintained despite the existence of this provision. Recommendation 6 of the RTPC report ends by recommending "that patents with respect to drugs be abolished. In the opinion of the Commission this is the only effective remedy to reduce the price of drugs in Canada."[23]

The RTPC investigation was followed by the 1965-67 Special Parliamentary Committee on Drug Costs and Prices, otherwise known as the Harley Committee. From the beginning this committee assumed that drug prices in Canada were too high. The terms of reference provided by cabinet stated "that the Committee be empowered to consider and recommend, as it may deem expedient, respecting a comprehensive and effective program to reduce the price of Drugs."[24] Following a series of public hearings the Harley Committee presented in 1967 a set of recommendations that were intended to form the basis for subsequent legislation, and its commitment to "reforming" the industry is apparent in the following summary of its salient recommendations:

(1)   That all medical and pharmacy students be instructed during their studies in the generic nomenclature for drugs.

(4)   That present ministerial authority as provided in section 30 of the Customs Act be amended insofar as the importation of drugs into Canada is concerned, and that future value for duty be set in all cases at the cost of production of the imported drug plus an allowance for gross profit (and an allowance to cover the actual manufacturer's administrative overheads, selling cost and net profit, etc.).

(5)   That the Customs Act be amended to make clear that dumping duties with respect to drugs be limited only to affect those drugs of a *kind* made in Canada.

(6)   That the federal government instruct the Tariff Board to revise the drug tariff structure.

(11)   That the Patent Commissioner on assessing royalties on the granting of a compulsory licence shall consider that the patentee who discovers and initially develops the drug in Canada should have higher royalties than the drug manufacturer who discovers new drugs outside of Canada.

(13)   That the federal sales tax be removed from the sale of prescription drugs.

(17)   That subsection (3) of section 41 of the Patent Act be amended to indicate already that the granting of a licence by the Commissioner of Patents is subject to a report by the Food and Drug Directorate of the Department of National Health and Welfare to the effect that the applicant for the compulsory licence has satisfied the Directorate that he has met the regulations under the Food and Drugs Act.

(18)   That subsection (3) of section 41 of the Patent Act be amended to include applications for compulsory licences to import drug

products in all forms subject to inspection of manufacturing facilities by the Food and Drug Directorate and provided such importation is in the public interest as may be determined by the Commissioner; and to this end, your committee recommends that the rules under the Patent Act be amended to permit the Commissioner to seek and receive outside independent expert advice in the determination of this question.

(20)   That subsection (3) of section 41 be amended so that if the granting of a compulsory licence takes longer than 12 months, the Commissioner, if in his opinion the delay is unwarranted, may be empowered to issue the licence subject to revocation if any appeal against such a compulsory licence is upheld, providing however that such licences provide sufficient evidence to satisfy standards of the Food and Drug Directorate.

(21)   That section 20 of the Trade Marks Act be amended to make clear that no infringement can be claimed where imported drugs are manufactured by a "related" company.

(23)   That the pharmaceutical industry abolish suggested list prices.[25]

A number of parliamentary acts were required to implement the recommendations, but the most important was Bill C-102, an "Act to Amend the Patent Act, the Trade Marks Act and the Food and Drugs Act," which went somewhat further than the Harley Committee may have intended. The act received Royal Assent on 22 June 1969, and with it Canada entered the era of compulsory drug licensing.[26]

It is noteworthy that many elements of Senator Kefauver's Bill S. 1552 were similar to recommendations of the Harley Committee. In particular, the former placed restrictions on advertising and required compulsory licensing (at an 8 per cent royalty rate) after only a short period of exclusive use by the patent holder.[27] The Pharmaceutical Manufacturers Association marshalled all its resources to fight these provisions of the Kefauver bill, and during its passage through Congress the bill was shorn of both of these provisions.

Similar suggestions were made in the U.K. at the time of the Sainsbury Committee, but they were never introduced into legislation. Instead, the industry and the government reached an agreement, called the Voluntary Price Regulation Scheme, under which the prices of drug products were negotiated between the industry and the Ministry of Health.[28] Clearly, the government could not allow uncontrolled drug prices when doctors and other suppliers of health services and products were under government control. Undoubtedly, there was accommodation on both sides because the industry had a substantial foreign trade balance, and because the leading firms in the industry were domestically owned.

It may be wondered why Canada did not reject compulsory licensing, when both the U.S. and the U.K. did. The opposition of the multinational industry to compulsory licensing in Canada was very strenuous, motivated by the fear that its adoption would set an example for other countries to follow.[29] However, in dealing with the government, the industry showed little sensitivity to the specific Canadian concerns that motivated the desire for change, insisting that Canadian legislation go no further than legislation in the U.S. The major factor, no doubt, in the industry's failure to prevent the enactment of compulsory licensing was the lack of Canadian-owned firms that could represent a "Canadian interest" in Ottawa and that had the familiarity with the local scene needed to negotiate effectively.

Performance of the Canadian Drug Industry in 1968

3

How does one evaluate the performance of an industry? As consumers, we judge an industry by the quality of its products and the prices charged: the lower the price—given the product's quality—the better the performance. On the other hand, as suppliers (of labour, material, capital, et cetera), we judge an industry by the prices it pays for our services. Furthermore, if our employment opportunities are limited, the higher the industry's level of employment—both in direct employment and in the indirect employment resulting from its material purchases—the better the industry's performance. The consumer and the supplier evaluations of an industry are referred to below as its price and expenditure performances, respectively.

Standard of Performance

To reach a conclusion on the price and expenditure performances of the Canadian drug industry, a standard of performance is needed. One such standard might be the value of these *Canadian* variables on some previous date. However, since our interest is in how well foreign ownership of the Canadian industry has served Canada, the appropriate standard of comparison should be a drug industry that is substantially free of foreign ownership. The U.S. drug industry seems best suited to fill this role for a number of reasons. First and foremost, it is by and large domestically owned. Secondly, the problems of obtaining the necessary data are less formidable for a U.S. industry than they would be for an industry of any other country. Thirdly, the Canadian and U.S. drug industries are similar in a number of important respects, such as the nature of medical practice, the type of drug products, and the standard of living of the consuming population.

It should be noted, however, that there are important differences between the two industries due to causes other than domestic versus foreign ownership—causes that include differences between the two countries in size, in economic development, and in the tax and other policies of their respective governments. Consequently, the comparative data presented below on prices, employment, rates of compensation and other such variables cannot provide a basis for reaching hard conclusions on how a domestically owned industry would perform for Canada. That is, we cannot infer from our comparison that domestic ownership would provide Canada with a scaled-down version of the U.S. industry. We can only speculate on what the performance of the Canadian industry would have been today if the government prior to the Second World War had adopted policies that fostered the further development of a domestically owned Canadian industry—or on what would happen if the government now were to adopt policies that would patriate ownership of the industry. In a subsequent chapter we do speculate on the possible consequences of reduced foreign ownership and of other changes in government policy.

If we can arrive at no hard conclusions, then what purpose is served by a comparison of the foreign-owned Canadian industry with the domestically owned U.S. industry? It has been argued that the U.S. multinational corporations bring to Canada, through their subsidiaries here, the benefits of their technological advances. If, as stated in chapter 1, 100 per cent success in the transfer of technology implies that the measures of performance should be the same in the two countries, then we may reasonably ask whether and to what degree the U.S. branch plants in Canada have achieved technology transfer. Clearly, the current performance of the Canadian vis-à-vis the U.S. industry is an important consideration in reaching a conclusion on the possible benefits to be derived from reducing foreign ownership or from following other policy options open to the government. An informed evaluation of these alternative policy options must be in terms of *current performance* and be based on information about the structure, organization and unique characteristics of the Canadian industry. Bear in mind that our objective is not domestic ownership—it is domestic performance.

We selected 1968 and 1976 as the two years for comparing the Canadian and American drug industries. We went back as far as 1968 because shortly thereafter the Canadian government adopted strong measures to reduce industry prices. These measures are described in the next chapter, which then presents comparative data for 1976 in order to show the impact that these government measures had on the performance of the Canadian drug industry.

Price Performance

Our desired measure of the price performance of the Canadian drug industry was the average price of drugs in Canada relative to the U.S. Since government agencies in both countries publish a great range of price indices, we expected to be able to obtain from these statistics, directly or indirectly, an index of drug prices in Canada vis-à-vis the U.S. That was not to be the case, however. Each country selects a representative sample of drugs, determines their prices over time, and derives thereby a time series of the country's average drug price. Unfortunately, the statistical agencies of the two countries do not arrive at identical drug samples to be priced, and furthermore, they did not consider themselves free to furnish us with their price and quantity data so that we could extract a *common* sample and price it in both countries for the years of interest to us.

We were able to obtain comparable price and quantity data for both Canada and the U.S. from IMS of Canada Ltd., a subsidiary of a worldwide organization that specializes in the collection of pharmaceutical industry data—including prices. The IMS data appears to be exceptionally reliable, since it is taken from customer invoices and not manufacturers' price lists. From this data we extracted a semi-random sample of 167 drugs and found that when prices were weighted by quantities sold, prices in Canada were 6 per cent lower than in the U.S. Canadian prices were 10 per cent higher when each drug was equally weighted. An exact description of how these price indices were developed is provided in the appendix.

A quantity-weighted index provides a superior measure of relative prices, and so it was somewhat surprising to find drug prices actually lower in Canada than in the U.S. The 10 per cent higher price level in Canada when drugs were equally weighted meant that prices in Canada were much higher on low-volume drugs and much lower on high-volume drugs. The explanation may be due, in part, to the fact that low-volume drugs were more likely to be produced outside Canada, and that there was a tariff (15 per cent for "most favoured nations") on drugs for which substitutes were not produced in Canada. However, since production costs in Canada were somewhat higher than in the U.S., they cannot explain the much lower prices in Canada for high-volume drugs.

Although these results may appear somewhat surprising, they are consistent with previous comparisons of drug prices in the two countries. A report to the Restrictive Trade Practices Commission revealed that in 1959 the prices of a number of drug products in Canada ranged from 18 per cent below to 54 per cent above their U.S. prices—and that Canadian drug prices were higher for a majority of the products surveyed.[1] A second study found that in 1966 drug prices were still higher in Canada than in the U.S.[2] Both of these studies, however, gave equal weight to all the sample drugs, substantiating our finding that when each drug is given an equal weight, the average price level is higher in Canada. It should be noted that our results are more reliable than those of the prior studies (insofar as the latter suggest that prices in Canada are more than 10 per cent higher when all drugs are equally weighted), because our prices were actual prices taken from manufacturers' invoices to pharmacists, while the earlier studies used manufacturers' list prices.

What remains to be explained is the substantially lower average price for high-volume drugs in Canada than in the U.S. One possible explanation is the existence of cooperative purchasing organizations to which Canadian pharmacists belong, enabling them to buy in large enough quantities to obtain much lower prices on high-volume drugs. However, we have no direct evidence on the effectiveness of these organizations. Another possibility is that the widespread investigation of the Canadian drug industry during the Sixties and the consideration of legislation to bring down drug prices—not merely to legislate more stringent testing standards—persuaded the drug firms to reduce their prices in an effort to head off such legislation.

The conclusion we reach is that drug prices in 1968 were about the same in the two countries, notwithstanding the fact that our quantity-weighted index showed drug prices to have been 6 per cent lower in Canada. First of all, our sample may not have given adequate weight to the large number of low-volume, patented drugs for which prices in Canada were higher. Secondly, an index of drug prices is subject to a much wider margin of error than most price indices, because production cost for drugs is, on average, very small in relation to price, and the prices of two essentially similar products may differ by 100 per cent or more—not by a maximum of 10 per cent as would be the case for most other products. It should be noted that our index is based on the manufacturers' average price to pharmacists, whereas the average price to the ultimate consumers depends in addition on the pharmacists' markups.

Expenditure Performance: Production Costs

Comparative Income Statements

A starting point for comparing the expenditure performances of the Canadian and the U.S. drug industries is provided by their 1968 condensed income statements as shown in Table 3-1. As explained in the appendix, the source of the data for this table is the census of manufactures for each country, and may, therefore, be considered quite reliable. Also, since the prices charged for drug products in the two countries are approximately the same, their respective data on volume of sales (real as well as nominal) are comparable.

The most striking feature of Table 3-1 is the difference it shows in production costs as percentages of sales. In Canada total production costs were 47 per cent of sales, while they were only 33 per cent in the U.S. The percentage costs for labour and energy were only slightly higher in the U.S., so that the difference in total costs is due entirely to material cost, which was 15.6 per cent higher in Canada.

Note that the gross-profit margin for the drug industry of each country was high, and especially so in the U.S., where it was 67 per cent. By comparison, the 1968 gross-profit margin for the U.S.

TABLE 3-1
CONDENSED INCOME STATEMENTS FOR THE CANADIAN AND U.S. DRUG INDUSTRIES, 1968
(millions of $'s)

	Canadian		U.S.	
	($)	(%)	($)	(%)
Sales	368.5	100.0	5,645.3	100.0
Production costs:				
Material	144.1	39.1	1,324.1	23.5
Fuel and electricity	2.0	.5	42.3	.7
Labour	27.0	7.4	494.4	8.8
Total	173.1	47.0	1,860.8	33.0
Gross profit	195.4	53.0	3,784.5	67.0

Source: See Appendix.

manufacturing sector as a whole (after adjusting for sales within the sector) was only 45.7 per cent, and for the U.S. textile industry it was only 19.8 per cent. As will be seen later, the high gross-profit margin for the drug industry of each country was largely absorbed by overhead costs, particularly research and development costs and the various components of selling expense.

Material Cost

A number of factors contributed to the large difference in material cost that existed between the Canadian and American drug industries in 1968. One of the factors was that in Canada the fraction of total sales that consisted of the resale of finished products manufactured elsewhere was much larger. Panel A of Table 3-2 reveals that resale products accounted for 11.6 per cent of Canadian sales in 1968,[3] while they only accounted for 2.4 per cent of U.S. sales, and panel B shows why this difference contributed to the higher material cost as a percentage of *aggregate* sales in Canada.

Material is the sole cost of sales for resale products. It was 82.5 per cent of sales in Canada, but only 58.2 per cent in the U.S. Canadian purchases for resale were all imports—largely from parent companies abroad, no doubt—so that practically the entire gross profit on Canada's resale products was taken by parent companies. In fact, Canada's 17.5 per cent gross margin on sales does not begin to cover its distribution, selling and general overhead expenses, so that the subsidiary companies experienced a large loss on their resale products. With resale a large fraction of sales in Canada and with the material cost of resale products almost equal to their sales value, resale contributed significantly to Canada's higher material cost as a fraction of sales. The effective duty on drug imports in 1968 was 10.5 per cent of the transfer price, so that the revenue to the parent on resale products averaged 74.7 per cent of the Canadian sales price.

Panel C of Table 3-2 compares for the two countries their 1968 income statements for products of own manufacture, and we see that the spread between them in material cost as a percentage of sales is much smaller than it was in Table 3-1, but it is still large: 33.4 per cent for Canada and 22.6 per cent for the U.S. The difference is due to a number of reasons that can be better understood if the nature and sources of materials employed in the manufacture of drugs, and the breakdown of material cost in panel C, are first explained.

The materials employed in the manufacture of drugs may be classified as: *active ingredients* (also called fine chemicals), which

46

TABLE 3-2
SALES AND CONDENSED INCOME STATEMENTS FOR THE CANADIAN AND U.S. DRUG INDUSTRIES, CLASSIFIED BY RESALE PRODUCTS AND PRODUCTS OF OWN MANUFACTURE, 1968
(millions of $'s)

	Canadian		U.S.	
	($)	(%)	($)	(%)
Classification of Sales by Type of Product				
Resale products	42.9	11.6	134.4	2.4
Products of own manufacture	325.6	88.4	5,510.9	97.6
Total	368.5	100.0	5,645.3	100.0
Income Statement for Resale Products				
Sales	42.9	100.0	134.4	100.0
Cost of sales				
Domestic material	—	—	10.0	7.4
Import material	35.4	82.5	68.2	50.8
Total	35.4	82.5	78.2	58.2
Gross profit	7.5	17.5	56.2	41.8
Income Statement for Products of Own Manufacture				
Sales	325.6	100.0	5,510.9	100.0
Production costs				
Material: drug imports	21.3	6.5	23.9	0.4
other imports	16.3	5.0	—	—
domestic materials	71.1	21.9	1,222.0	22.2
Sub total	108.7	33.4	1,245.9	22.6
Fuel and electricity	2.0	0.6	42.3	0.8
Labour	27.0	8.3	494.4	9.0
Total	137.7	42.3	1,782.6	32.4
Gross Profit	187.9	57.7	3,728.3	67.6

ce: See Appendix.

provide therapeutic benefits; *inert ingredients*, which provide bulk, dispersion, taste and other ancillary properties; and *packaging materials*, such as containers and labels. Drug firms in the U.S. manufactured practically all of the active ingredients they required, while in Canada practically all active ingredients were imported from parent companies abroad. As for inert ingredients and packaging materials, Canada purchased them both at home and abroad, whereas in the U.S. they were nearly all purchased domestically.

The material cost on products of own manufacture in panel C of Table 3-2 are classified as drug imports, other imports, and domestic materials. This breakdown is explained in the appendix. If the tariff on drug imports were 10.5 per cent on average, and if the tariff on other imports were 15.0 per cent on average, eliminating the tariff would reduce the cost of materials from 33.4 to 32.1 per cent of sales, a figure that is still much higher than the 22.6 per cent in the U.S.

Let us now examine why material cost on products of own manufacture was so much larger a percentage of sales in Canada in 1968 than it was in the U.S. To the extent that Canadian firms imported intermediate materials, while U.S. firms acquired raw materials at home, the Canadian material cost was inflated to reflect the gross margins on its imports. For intermediate materials imported from foreign parents, the gross margins would be the very high margins that are typical of the drug industry and that are only possible in parent-subsidiary sales. For materials other than drugs, the prices paid would reflect the smaller margins that are usually enjoyed by other industries and that take place in arm's-length transactions between independent companies. A reasonable assumption is that the production cost of the materials imported by Canadian firms was 50 per cent of the prices paid. Hence, these imports probably accounted for about half of the 10.8 per cent difference in material costs between Canada and the U.S. that is shown in panel C of Table 3-2.[4]

Panel C shows that the cost of materials acquired domestically was about the same percentage of sales in Canada as it was in the U.S.: 21.9 and 22.2 per cent, respectively. Since a substantial fraction of Canada's material requirements was satisfied by imports, its domestic purchases should have been a substantially smaller fraction of sales than was the case for the U.S.—if all else had been the same. However, there is reason to believe that everything else was not the same. It is widely accepted that for various reasons chemicals and packaging materials sold at higher prices in Canada than in the U.S. Also, production runs were smaller in Canadian subsidiaries than they were in U.S. firms. When production is in small batches with extremely high standards of quality control, material usage will be higher. For Canada, smaller output volumes also meant smaller purchase quantities and somewhat higher unit prices. These sources of comparative inefficiency in Canada probably explain about half of the 10.8 per cent difference in material cost on drugs of own manufacture between Canada and the U.S.

In conclusion, this large difference in material cost as a percentage of sales between the two countries in 1968 was due to a number of factors, the most obvious being:

- the large import of resale products by Canadian subsidiaries and the very low gross-profit margin that they are allowed to earn on imports;
- the high gross margin to the manufacturer on imported drugs in semi-finished form—drugs that are largely manufactured by parent companies abroad;
- the higher prices paid for materials in Canada than in the U.S., with other things the same;
- the still higher material prices in Canada due to the smaller purchase quantities;
- the higher material usage due to the small production runs;
- the tariff.

It is our rough estimate that 60 per cent of the 15.6 per cent difference in Table 3-1 was due to the gross margin on imports, 27 per cent was due to the higher prices paid for materials in Canada, and 13 per cent was due to the tariff.

Labour Cost

Looking back at Table 3-1, we see that labour cost of production in Canada was lower than in the U.S.: 7.4 versus 8.8 per cent. With the elimination of resale products (which require no production labour), we see in Table 3-2 that the respective percentages become 8.3 and 9.0, a substantially smaller spread. However, this does not mean that production in Canada is more efficient in the use of labour. Production in the U.S. begins with the manufacture of fine chemicals, while Canadian production only involves mixing, pelletizing and packaging of the ingredients. In addition, the more difficult drugs are completely produced in the U.S. We would, therefore, expect an even larger gap between the two countries in their costs of production labour.

TABLE 3-3
EMPLOYMENT, COMPENSATION AND PRODUCTIVITY OF PRODUCTION WORKERS IN THE CANADIAN AND U.S. DRUG INDUSTRIES, 1968

	Canadian	U.S.		Ratio: U.S./Cdn
	(a)	(b)	(c)	(c/a)
Total production hours (000)	11,085	130,700		11.79
	(Cdn $)	(U.S. $)	(Cdn $)	
Total compensation of production workers (000)	26,995	494,400	534,486	19.43
Hourly compensation	2.44	3.78	4.09	1.68
Total value of output (000)	325,600	5,510,900	5,957,700	18.30
Value of output per production hour	29.37	42.16	45.58	1.55

Source: See Appendix.

More information on the difference between the two countries in cost of production labour as a percentage of sales is provided by their 1968 production hours, compensation of production workers, and other such data in Table 3-3. Dividing the compensation of production workers by production hours reveals that the hourly compensation rate (after adjusting for the exchange rate) was 68 per cent higher in the U.S. Therefore, if all else were the same, we would expect to find that the cost of production labour in Canada was about 40 per cent lower than in the U.S. However, we did not find all else the same. In particular, U.S. drug workers were considerably more productive than workers in the Canadian industry. The value of output per production worker was only $29.37 in Canada, while it was equal to $45.58 (Canadian), or 55 per cent higher, in the U.S. In fact, the difference in productivity was even larger than these figures would indicate, since the U.S. industry acquired materials at an earlier stage in the production process. It should be noted that the above figures for value of output are comparable, since product prices were about equal in the two countries. To summarize, the wages of production workers as a percentage of sales were only slightly higher in the U.S. than in Canada, because the much higher wage rate per worker in the U.S. was largely offset by the much higher output per production worker there.

Why were output per worker and the hourly wage rate both so much higher in the U.S. than in Canada? In regard to output per worker, it would be wrong to attribute the difference of over 55 per cent to greater skill or productivity on the part of U.S. workers. The most skilled tool-and-die maker need be no more productive than a completely unskilled labourer if both are given a pick and shovel and told to dig a hole in the ground. In other words, differences between the two countries in the nature and scale of the production process, rather than differences in the skill or energy of their workers, is probably the major explanation for the large difference in output per worker.[5] As for the higher average wage rate in the U.S., it was due in part to the greater skill content and higher hourly wage rates of the jobs provided by the U.S. drug industry, but it was also due in part to the generally higher wage rates in the U.S. For all manufacturing, the 1968 average hourly wage rate was $2.55 in Canada and $3.35 (Canadian), or 31 per cent higher, in the U.S. However, this substantial wage difference between the two countries did not, it would appear, lead to any considerable establishment of plants to produce for export to the U.S. and elsewhere. Canada's net export of drugs in 1968 was only $15.4 million, of which 25 per cent was attributable to just one firm, Connaught Laboratories, which was the only important domestically owned pharmaceutical company in Canada.[6]

Although the compensation rate of $2.44 per hour in the Canadian drug industry was slightly lower than the $2.55 average for all Canadian manufacturing, it was nonetheless, quite attractive. The work is light and the physical environment is pleasant. Furthermore, the pay scale in the drug industry can be considered higher than for manufacturing in general, because a large fraction of the drug industry's workers are women and the average pay scale for women in manufacturing is substantially below that for men. For comparison, in textiles, where a large fraction of the production workers were also women, the average wage rate was $1.95 per hour.

Expenditure Performance: Overhead Costs

The 1968 distribution of gross profits for the Canadian and American drug industries is presented in Table 3-4. It was not possible to obtain a breakdown of overhead costs from the census data, and the additional

TABLE 3-4
DISTRIBUTION OF GROSS PROFITS FOR THE CANADIAN AND U.S. DRUG INDUSTRIES, 1968
(millions of $'s)

	Canadian		U.S.	
	Dollar Amount	Per Cent of Sales	Dollar Amount	Per Cent of Sales
Gross profit	195.37	53.0	3,784.5	67.0
Overhead costs				
Cost of research and development				
Payroll	6.57	1.8	253.3	4.5
Purchased services	4.35	1.2	170.0	3.0
Subtotal	10.92	3.0	423.3	7.5
Salary compensation other than R&D	54.78	14.9	592.2	10.5
Non-payroll selling expenses				
Travel and entertainment	26.31	7.1	120.2	2.1
Advertising and promotion	27.75	7.5	570.7	10.1
Subtotal	54.06	14.6	690.9	12.2
Purchased business services	17.47	4.7	225.4	4.0
Depreciation expense	6.11	1.7	116.9	2.1
Other overhead costs	25.13	6.8	364.4	6.5
Total overhead costs	168.47	45.7	2,413.1	42.8
Income taxes	13.79	3.7	617.1	10.9
Net profit after taxes	13.11	3.6	754.3	13.3

Source: See Appendix

sources used did not provide the desired detail in a consistent manner. Consequently, as explained in the appendix, there is some margin of error in the allocation of the costs in Table 3-4.

Costs of Research and Development

The interest of government agencies in research and development expenditures results in data that is probably quite accurate. In 1968 such expenditures were 3 per cent of sales in Canada, while they were more than double that in the U.S. These figures, however, fail to reveal the differences that exist between the two countries in the nature of their R&D activity. R&D in the drug industry falls under four major headings:

- the discovery of new drugs—or of improvements to existing drugs—and their testing on nonhuman subjects;
- an initial program of human testing that is extremely careful and highly controlled to detect any undesirable health effects;
- an extensive program of human testing to secure approval of the new drug by an appropriate government agency in some major country;
- additional testing to secure adoption of the drug in other countries.

R&D activity in the U.S. falls under all four of these categories, but primarily under the first three. In Canada R&D is mainly confined to the testing required to secure adoption of new drugs after their adoption in another country.

Typically, drugs introduced into Canada have been previously approved in the U.S., England or elsewhere, and the foreign test results are used in the Canadian submission. Testing is normally done in Canada only to the extent that the regulatory agency requires additional evidence. Whether additional testing reflects higher acceptance standards in Canada, or a form of "featherbedding" indulged in by government agencies, is a matter of some dispute.[7] Regardless, it represents the entire R&D activity of most drug firms in Canada.

Certain observations made to us about the quality and quantity of R&D carried out by the Canadian subsidiaries of multinational corporations led us to believe that their expenditure on R&D as a percentage of sales would be far less than one-half the U.S. percentage. We were told that only Connaught and Ayerst did significant R&D work and, furthermore, that all but a few of the multinational subsidiaries established here did no research on product development and the testing they did was the minimum required to introduce into Canada products established elsewhere. We sent a questionnaire on the subject to every firm of note in the industry, but the response level was so low that the replies we did obtain were useless.

Further investigation of R&D expenditures in 1968 revealed the following. First, Connaught Laboratories, with sales of $8,839,000, had R&D expenditures of $2,138,000, or 24 per cent of sales.[8] Thus Connaught, with 2.5 per cent of industry sales, accounted for 19.6 per cent of the industry's R&D expenditures. Secondly, two of the largest firms in the industry, Ayerst and Merck Frosst (both of which were domestically owned before being acquired by U.S. firms) had combined R&D expenditures in 1968 that were almost certainly in excess of $5 million.

We may deduce that the R&D expenditures of the subsidiaries that were established here (firms other than Connaught, Ayerst, and Merck Frosst) were less than $3.9 million, or only about 1 per cent of their combined sales, and, furthermore, that practically none of this expenditure was on new product development or primary testing.[9] Hence, the most generous thing one can say about the multinational presence in Canada up to 1968 was that in acquiring Canadian companies they did not destroy the existing R&D organizations. Practically nothing by way of R&D activity was introduced to Canada through the subsidiaries of the multinationals that were established here. The dollar amount of the expenditures was trivial, and the qualitative level of the research was even lower.

Costs of Salary Compensation Other than R&D

Included here in the costs of salary compensation other than R&D are the costs of all personnel (sales, managerial, clerical, warehouse) other than those engaged in R&D and production. The salary cost of these other employees was 14.9 per cent of sales in Canada, but it was only 10.5 per cent in the U.S. One would expect this difference to have been in the opposite direction, since Canadian subsidiaries have limited managerial responsibilities. However, there are two reasons for the higher percentage cost in Canada: (1) a much higher level in Canada of selling activity and expenditures in relation to sales than in the U.S. (this will be discussed shortly); and (2) a comparative inefficiency in the use of salaried employees in Canada.

TABLE 3-5
EMPLOYMENT, COMPENSATION AND SALES PER EMPLOYEE FOR SALARIED EMPLOYEES IN THE CANADIAN AND U.S. DRUG INDUSTRIES, 1968

	Canadian	U.S.		Ratio: U.S./Cdn
	(a)	(b)	(c)	(c/a)
Number of salaried employees	7,325	70,500		9.62
	(Cdn $)	(U.S. $)	(Cdn $)	
Total compensation of salaried employees (000)	61,355	865,200	935,351	15.24
Average compensation	8,372	12,272	13,267	1.58
Total sales (000)	368,500	5,645,300	6,103,027	16.56
Sales per salaried employee	50,280	80,075	86,568	1.72

Source: See Appendix.

The data in Table 3-5, which is analogous to the data on production workers in Table 3-3, shows that the 1968 compensation per salaried employee was $8,372 in Canada, while it was $13,267, or 58 per cent higher, in the U.S. This difference was due both to the higher rate of compensation per salary grade in the U.S. and to the higher status of the U.S. employment opportunities in the drug industry. In spite of this, however, the cost of salaried employees *per sales dollar* was higher in Canada (14.9 per cent versus 10.5 per cent) due to the much higher volume of sales per salaried employee in the U.S. The volume for Canada was $50,280 compared to $86,568 for the U.S.

Consequently, we see that in 1968 salaried as well as production workers had much lower levels of "productivity" and rates of compensation in Canada than they had in the U.S., primarily because in Canada there was: (1) a lower level of management responsibilities and functions; and (2) a larger number of small drug firms, resulting in both higher overhead costs and higher sales expenditures per dollar of sales.

TABLE 3-6
PERCENTAGE DISTRIBUTION OF EMPLOYEES BY TYPE OF OCCUPATION IN THE CANADIAN (1970) AND U.S. (1971) DRUG INDUSTRIES
(%)

Type of Occupation	Canadian	U.S.
Engineers, scientists and other technicians	14.14	21.16
Managers	9.10	10.96
Salespersons	18.20	9.74
Clerical persons	25.16	20.12
Production workers	23.72	23.15
Craft, service and other workers	9.68	14.87
Total	100.00	100.00

Source: See Appendix.

More information on the differences in employment opportunities between Canadian and U.S. drug industries is to be found in Table 3-6, which presents the percentage distribution of all employees by type of occupation—for Canada in 1970 and for the U.S. in 1971. As one would expect, a materially smaller fraction of the Canadian employees were technical workers: 14.14 per cent compared to 21.16 per cent for the U.S. The fraction of employees classified as managerial was also lower in Canada: 9.10 per cent versus 10.96 per cent. However, in Canada 18.20 per cent of the employees were in sales as compared with only 9.74 per cent in the U.S. Canada also had a larger fraction of its employees engaged in clerical functions: 25.16 per cent versus 20.12 per cent. It is also interesting to note that while production workers represented about 23 per cent of all employees in both countries, workers engaged in craft and service occupations represented only 9.68 per cent of all employees in Canada, but 14.87 per cent in the U.S. In conclusion, we see that for both blue-collar and white-collar employees, the fraction of the labour force in the more skilled and desirable jobs was higher in the U.S. than in Canada.

Selling Expenses

Selling expenses consist of the compensation paid employees engaged in selling and marketing activities, and the non-payroll selling expenses presented in Table 3-4: travel and entertainment, and advertising and promotion. There is no breakdown of the category, "salary compensation other than R&D," to show the compensation of employees engaged in selling, but the data in Table 3-6 on the percentage distribution of employees by type of occupation makes it clear that the fraction of the sales dollar spent on compensation of salespersons was much higher in Canada than in the U.S. From that and other data we estimate that the cost was 5.2 per cent of sales in Canada, but only 2.5 per cent in the U.S. As can be seen in Table 3-4, non-payroll selling expenses as a percentage of sales were also higher in Canada: 14.6 per cent versus 12.2 per cent in the U.S. Combining these figures with the previous 5.2 and 2.5 leads to the conclusion that selling expenses in 1968 were about 20 per cent of sales in Canada compared to 15 per cent in the U.S.[10]

There are two possible explanations for Canada's higher level of selling expenses in relation to sales. First, the firms are small and the country is large, both of which probably require a larger sales expenditure per dollar of sales in Canada than in the U.S. Secondly, many drug firms had come to Canada only recently. They were engaging in extraordinary sales efforts during the late Sixties in order to introduce new products into the Canadian market. It has been found that sales expenses are an extraordinarily large fraction of sales, sometimes over 50 per cent, when a new product is introduced.[11]

Other Overhead Costs

The remaining overhead costs (purchased business services, depreciation expense, and others) differed only slightly between the two countries. However, purchased business services for the Canadian industry, including royalty payments, consulting fees and management fees, were in large measure payments to foreign parents.

Profit and Income Tax Performance

A striking difference between the two industries in 1968 was in the much larger fraction of sales revenue in the U.S. that went to income taxes and to net profit after taxes. For taxes, the U.S. percentage was about three times larger than the Canadian, and for net profit after taxes, the percentage were 13.3 per cent versus 3.6 per cent. Canada has no interest in net profit after taxes, since foreign ownership makes it flow abroad. However, net profit before taxes, which was 24.2 per cent in the U.S. and 7.3 per cent in Canada, is of considerable interest because it determines the income tax revenues that flow to the Canadian government.

A number of factors contributed to the very much lower profitability of the Canadian industry. One reason was the exceptional sales effort that was made around 1968 to develop the Canadian market. However, a reduction in selling expenses to achieve the same relative level as in the U.S. industry would have raised profits before taxes by only 5 per cent of sales. Another reason for the lower profit rate in Canada was undoubtedly the generally higher cost of overhead and production activities. Finally, the difference in relative profitability was due in part to the terms under which resale products, raw materials, and business services were transferred from foreign parents to Canadian subsidiaries. The terms were designed to transfer profits out of the Canadian subsidiaries. Clearly, this was the case for resale products, where the transfer prices were on average 82.5 per cent of the selling prices. The 17.5 per cent gross margin, however, in no way covered the selling and other overhead expenses incurred by the Canadian subsidiaries.

Unfortunately, it is not possible to arrive at a transfer price that correctly allocates the pretax net profit on Canadian sales between parent and subsidiary. A transfer price equal to only the parent's production costs would not cover a fair share of the parent's other costs (for R&D, general management, et cetera), and the high profits on drug products are due in large measure to these other activities that are carried on by the *parent* company. On the other hand, there is no problem in determining the pretax net profit that the subsidiary contributes to the parent. It includes: (1) the pretax net profit that appears in the subsidiary's accounts; (2) the excess of the transfer price over the parent's production costs; and (3) the parent-to-subsidiary charges for royalties and business services. In 1968, the average net profit before taxes that appeared in the accounts of Canadian subsidiaries was 7.3 per cent of their sales. Transfer pricing captured about 5.8 per cent of total sales for resale products and about 2.8 per cent for fine chemicals.[12] Next, for business services the parents charged the subsidiaries about 2.9 per cent of the Canadian sales (see Table 3-7 and the discussion below). And, finally, if we add on the 5 per cent by which Canadian selling activity exceeded the U.S. level,

58

TABLE 3-7

ALLOCATION OF REVENUES FROM THE CANADIAN DRUG INDUSTRY BETWEEN CANADIAN AND FOREIGN RECIPIENTS, 1968

(thousands of $'s)

	Canadian Recipients		Foreign Recipients	
	(Cdn $)	(%)	(Cdn $)	(%)
Material cost	71.2	19.3	65.5	17.8
Import tariff	7.5	2.0		
Fuel and electricity	2.0	0.5		
Production labour	27.0	7.4		
Cost of research and development	7.1	2.0	3.8	1.0
Salary compensation other than R&D	54.8	14.9		
Non-payroll selling expenses	54.0	14.6		
Purchased business services	6.7	1.8	10.8	2.9
Depreciation expense	6.1	1.7		
Other overhead costs	25.1	6.8		
Income taxes	13.8	3.7		
Net profit after taxes	0.2	0.0	12.9	3.5
Total	275.5	74.7	93.0	25.3

Source: See Appendix.

we see that the pretax net profit contributed to foreign parents by the Canadian drug industry was equal to 23.8 per cent of Canadian sales, and that percentage is about equal to the percentage earned by the parent companies on their own sales—in spite of the higher production costs borne by the Canadian subsidiaries.

Tax considerations will influence a multinational corporation on the amount of profit it will recognize in a subsidiary's accounts and on the amount it will not recognize by means of transfer pricing and charges for business services. Insofar as the Canadian drug industry is *actually* less profitable than the U.S., it could be expected to generate less tax revenues as a percentage of sales, but that cannot explain the 1968 spread of 3.74 to 10.93 per cent. This significant spread was also due to the use of transfer prices to reduce *reported* profits, since the effective tax rate in Canada was somewhat higher than in the U.S. and considerably higher than in other countries. Finally, it should be noted that the U.S. profit and tax figures are for U.S. output only, including the relatively small amounts that go to subsidiaries of foreign (mainly English, Swiss and German) companies operating in the U.S., and excluding the relatively large amounts that go to U.S. companies from their subsidiaries abroad.

Conclusion: Technology Transfer

On the basis of the above comparison of the Canadian and U.S. drug industries, we may now reach certain conclusions regarding the extent to which foreign ownership of the Canadian industry involved technology transfer in 1968. We have seen that as customers of the industry, Canadians enjoyed products of the same quality at comparable prices,[13] but when we turn to the transfer to Canada of the activities carried out by the U.S. and other foreign corporations, we cannot escape the conclusion that practically nothing has been accomplished. The high-technology manufacture of the fine chemicals remained abroad. The secondary manufacturing operations carried out in the Canadian industry were quite inefficient, and the methods of production were widely known in Canada without the presence of the multinational corporations. The specific formulae for the manufacture of each product were developed abroad and provided to the subsidiaries. The research and development work in Canada was not similar to the work carried out abroad: it merely served to meet the marketing problems of introducing into Canada products that were developed and first introduced abroad. The multinational corporations did introduce into Canada the selling and promotional practices developed abroad,

60

but the Canadian sales organizations were divisional in character and did not include top level staff organizations to design and initiate new marketing strategies.

The above conclusions were not true of every Canadian subsidiary. They did not describe Ayerst or Merck Frosst, but this only meant that the transfer of their ownership abroad did not result in stripping them of the technology they had previously developed. The above conclusions also did not describe a few subsidiaries, such as Ortho, which were introduced into Canada by foreign multinationals. Nonetheless, the most distinguished Canadian firm in R&D activities and in the technology of manufacturing was the one firm owned in Canada—Connaught Laboratories.

Setting aside the qualitative nature of the activities carried on by the Canadian industry, let us now turn to a quantitative evaluation of its expenditure performance. The 1968 allocation of the Canadian sales dollar between domestic and foreign beneficiaries is presented in Table 3-7. In that table, the allocation of material cost is based on the data in Table 3-2. R&D expenditures and purchased business services are allocated on the basis of CALURA (Corporations and Labour Unions Returns Act) statistics. Practically all of net profit after taxes was allocated to foreign beneficiaries, because foreign-owned corporations earned almost all of the profits of the Canadian drug industry. (In 1976 they earned 98.9 per cent, and their percentage was probably about the same in 1968.) Adding up the percentages in the two columns of Table 3-7 reveals that a large fraction of the sales dollar, 74.7 per cent, was expended on Canadian goods and services[14]—notwithstanding the predominance of foreign ownership for the industry and the extremely low level of the activities carried on in Canada by the subsidiaries.

However, some of the reasons for this fraction being so large are not very satisfying. First, marketing activities have to be carried out in Canada, and 20 per cent of the sales dollar was spent on marketing activities. Secondly, the inefficiency of the industry in Canada required a higher level of employment and expenditure to carry out a given level of activity. Ideally, these activities should have been carried out with fewer people at a somewhat higher rate of compensation, and other activities such as fine chemical production and R&D should have been located here. More efficiency without additional activity only increases the profits that flow abroad. Finally, the figures that give rise to the 74.7 per cent include Connaught, Ayerst, and Merck Frosst; the fraction of the sales dollar spent in Canada for subsidiaries *introduced into* Canada would be somewhat smaller.

61

Performance in 1976: The Impact of Competition Policy

4

During the Sixties the drug industry was investigated by government commissions in the U.S., Canada and elsewhere. These investigations reached the conclusion that industry prices and profits, particularly prices, were exorbitant and that a primary cause of the exorbitant prices was excessive marketing expenditures that were designed to suppress competition. The industry responded that the introduction of new drugs had provided tremendous benefits in terms of improved health, that these new drugs required very large expenditures on R&D, that marketing expenditures were needed to introduce new drugs to doctors, and that the industry could not perform its vital function without the seemingly high prices and high *gross-profit* margins needed to cover these costs.[1]

The initial impetus for the Canadian investigations was provided by informal complaints to the director of investigation and research of the RTPC about the high cost of drugs. The price situation had become an increasingly sensitive issue, because the federal and provincial governments had been providing a substantial and increasing fraction of the cost of health care in Canada, and both levels of government had adopted competition policies aimed at reducing the cost of drugs. The following section describes these measures, the next examines their impact on the prices charged for drugs, and the remainder of the chapter examines the impact of this competition policy on the demand/expenditure performance of the industry. For this analysis, 1976 was selected for comparison with 1968 because it is the most recent year for which all the data we might employ was available for both the U.S. and the Canadian industries.

Competition Policy

Several legislative initiatives at both the federal and provincial levels have had a significant impact on the competitiveness of the Canadian industry. In 1969 the federal government adopted legislation that compelled a manufacturer of a patented drug to grant a license to any firm that requested it—subject to a modest royalty payment. Under this legislation the licensed firm did not have to manufacture the product in Canada; it could import either the product or the fine chemicals, just so long as the final pharmaceutical preparation was made in Canada.

The first compulsory license was issued by Hoffmann-La Roche to Frank W. Horner, and covered the right to market diazepam, a tranquilizer sold under the trade name Valium. The royalty rate was set at 4 per cent, a figure that became established as the norm for future licensees.

But a license to sell a patented drug product was only the first step. The licensed firm also had to obtain approval for its substitute drug from the Health Protection Branch of the Department of National Health and Welfare. More important, it had to overcome the strong brand-name identification the original producer had acquired. Since doctors typically use brand names rather than generic names in writing prescriptions, it was necessary for the licensed firm to establish its own brand name if it was to gain a position in the market. Thus we see that compulsory licensing was only a small step—even though a key one—toward increasing the competitiveness of the drug market. The barriers to entry posed by the brand-name products were sufficiently discouraging that few compulsory licenses were issued until legislation was enacted to deal with this problem.

Well before 1969 the RTPC *Report* had not only condemned the use of trade names but had also suggested means whereby doctors could be made more aware of drug prices. To improve the situation, the Department of National Health and Welfare started in 1970 to publish the *Rx Bulletin*, a monthly listing of drugs that had been tested by the Health Protection Branch for identity, assay, weight variation, and other properties. Drugs that passed were listed by group under a generic heading and ranked in ascending order of price. The 1970 Parcost program in Ontario had a similar aim: to sensitize doctors and the consuming public to differences in drug prices. It publishes a *Drug Benefit Formulary*, which lists all drugs approved for reimbursement in the province and identifies the different brands of a drug that are considered acceptable substitutes for the original patented product.[2]

The above steps, however, were merely forms of moral suasion, which had little effect on the prescribing habits of physicians or the dispensing habits of pharmacists. A number of steps were taken to remedy the situation:

- The *Compilation of the Drug Quality Assessment Program* was published to "assure" the quality of tested drugs so that doctors could prescribe the cheapest available product. Although the doctor is not absolved from liability should the tested product prove harmful, the compilation did increase confidence in the generic substitutes.
- The Ontario Pharmacy Act was amended to allow a pharmacist to substitute any interchangeable drug from those listed in the *Formulary* for a prescribed one—unless the doctor had specifically forbidden any substitution—and the act protected the pharmacist from legal responsibility for making the substitution.
- On all prescriptions paid for by the province, the pharmacist is reimbursed at the lowest list price in the *Formulary*.

Notice that the pharmacist is not required to dispense the least expensive product, and on privately paid prescriptions the pharmacist need not price the prescription on the basis of the least expensive product.

However, compulsory licensing and product selection (generic substitution by the pharmacist) did not result in a flood of competition and a widespread fall in prices. Although the large established firms that manufacture the original products have the resources to engage in effective generic competition with each other, they, in fact, follow a policy of not obtaining compulsory licenses or engaging in price competition. The entry of new firms into the industry proved difficult to accomplish. First, the personnel and the facilities (manufacturing and quality control) they needed to manufacture the product had to be established. Secondly, a source of supply for the fine chemical ingredients had to be found. Finally, federal and provincial approval of their facilities and of each product had to be obtained, requiring some human testing, paper work, and time.

The Health Protection Branch has taken administrative steps to simplify somewhat the approval procedure for additional suppliers of a drug. For example, one of the primary requirements for obtaining approval of a drug product is to determine the toxicity of its basic chemical entity—a fairly complex, expensive and time-consuming process that involves feeding the material to several species of animals and establishing mortality rates. Now, under current regulations, the first supplier of a drug product must carry out these tests, but subsequent applicants may use these results, providing that the chemical entities are identical. This simplification is clearly designed to reduce entry barriers and encourage new firms to enter the market.

The most formidable task the would-be generic producer faces is the sale of the product. Only in Saskatchewan does the lowest quoted price provide that producer with a provincial market. In Ontario and Quebec the pharmacist may buy and dispense any of the listed products, but on prescriptions paid for by the province reimbursement is at the lowest list price. On prescriptions paid for by the consumer, it is certainly considered ethical for the pharmacist to dispense the prescribed brand and charge a price based on its list price. Thus, it is possible for the brand-name manufacturers to adopt marketing strategies that preserve a large fraction of the market for their products. For instance, they can offer volume discounts that reduce the effective prices below their list prices, thereby making it more profitable for the pharmacist to dispense their products on private prescriptions—and perhaps, on provincially reimbursed prescriptions as well.

We see, then, that the costs of entry and the barriers to market penetration limit the extent to which generic producers provide effective competition. At the time of writing, there were only four generic suppliers in Canada of any consequence.[3] More important, these four have found it profitable to offer generic competition on only a limited number of products—where the sales volume is large and where the basic fine chemicals are available on the open market. As shown in Table 4-1, by 1976 there had been little relative increase in the activity of domestically controlled firms. In fact, both production and nonproduction employment in Canadian establishments actually declined as a percentage of total employment. Shipments of products of own manufacture by Canadian-owned firms increased from 14.1 to 16.2 per cent, but the increase for total shipments was probably negative, since the shipments of resale products by foreign subsidiaries increased as a fraction of total shipments.

Perhaps the most effective and dramatic description of the industry may be provided by reproducing information from one page of Ontario's *Drug Benefit Formulary*, as is done in Table 4-2. Reading across any row, we have the generic name, the quantity, the brand name, the acronym for the manufacturer, and the manufacturer's list price. Where two or more brand names appear opposite a generic name, the pharmacist may dispense any of the brands. However, on prescriptions paid for by the province, reimbursement will be at the lowest price, shown in boldface type. Note the wide range in the prices for propoxyphene, where Darvon-N, the brand-name product, is not 20 or 30 per cent more expensive than the least expensive generic

TABLE 4-1
COMPARISON OF PHARMACEUTICAL ESTABLISHMENTS OPERATING IN CANADA UNDER FOREIGN AND DOMESTIC CONTROL, 1969 and 1976
(%)

| | Under Foreign Control | | | | | | Under Domestic Control | |
| | United States | | European | | Total | | | |
	(1969)	(1976)	(1969)	(1976)	(1969)	(1976)	(1969)	(1976)
Number of establishments	34.7	40.1	8.0	9.0	42.7	49.1	57.3	50.7
Number of production workers	61.2	61.3	10.5	11.6	71.7	72.9	28.3	27.1
Total production wages	63.5	63.4	10.8	11.2	74.3	74.6	25.7	25.4
Number of nonproduction employees	69.9	67.4	14.1	18.9	84.0	86.3	16.0	13.7
Total salaries	71.2	67.8	14.1	19.7	85.3	87.5	14.7	12.5
Shipment of goods of own manufacture	72.5	68.4	13.4	15.4		83.8	14.1	16.2
Value added from manufacturing	74.5	72.7	13.0	14.7		87.4	12.5	12.6

Sources: Statistics Canada, *Domestic and Foreign Control of Manufacturing Establishments in Canada, 1969 and 1970* (Ottawa: 1976), p. 64; Statistics Canada, *Domestic and Foreign Control of Manufacturing Establishments in Canada, 1976* (Ottawa: 1981), pp. 34-35.

TABLE 4-2
EXCERPTED MANUFACTURERS' LIST PRICES FOR CERTAIN DRUGS IN ONTARIO, EFFECTIVE 1 JANUARY 1981

Generic Name/Quantity	Brand Name	Manu-facturer	List Price
Analgesics			
Propoxyphene Cap	Pro-65	ICN	**0.0270**
	Novopropoxyn	NOP	0.0285
	Propoxyphene	SAP	0.0378
	Darvon-N	LIL	0.0751
Sulindac 200mg Tab	Clinoril	FRS	**0.3602**
Sulindac 150mg Tab	Clinoril	FRS	**0.2840**
Tolmetin Sodium 200mg Tab	Tolectin	MCN	**0.1310**
Tolmetin Sodium 400mg Cap	Tolectin DS	MCN	**0.2382**
Narcotic Antagonists			
Levallorphan Tartrate 1mg/ml Inj Sol 1ml Pk	Lorfan	HLR	**0.9218**
Naloxone HCI 0.4mg/ml Inj Sol 1ml Pk	Narcan	END	**2.8875**
Anticonvulsants			
Carbamazepine 200mg Tab	Apo-Carbamazepine	APX	**0.1295**
	Tegretol	GEI	0.1542
Clonazepam 2mg Tab	Rivotril	HLR	**0.1441**
Clonazepam 0.5mg Tab	Rivotril	HLR	**0.0831**
Ethosuximide 250mg Cap	Zarontin	PDA	**0.1236**
Ethosuximide 50mg/ml O/L	Zarontin	PDA	**0.0284**
Mephenytoin 100mg Tab	Mesantoin	SAN	**0.0539**
Mephobarbital 200mg Tab	Mebaral	WIN	**0.0925**
Mephobarbital 100mg Tab	Mebaral	WIN	**0.0595**
Methsuximide 300mg Cap	Celontin	PDA	**0.1459**
Paramethadione 300mg Cap	Paradione	ABB	**0.1201**
Phenobarbital 100mg Tab	Phenobarbital	ANC	**0.0137**
	Phenobarbital	DTC	0.0140
Phenobarbital 60mg Tab	Phenobarbital	DTC	**0.0090**
	Phenobarbital	PDA	0.0108
Phenobarbital 300mg Tab	Phenobarbital	ANC	**0.0046**
	Phenobarbital	DTC	0.0048
	Phenobarbital	PDA	0.0057

Source: *Drug Benefit Formulary*, No. 14, ISSN 0319-0056 (Toronto: Province of Ontario, 1981), p. 39.

substitute, Pro-65—it is almost 300 per cent more expensive and, undoubtedly, has most of the market. Note also the large number of products for which there are no generic substitutes.

Impact on Prices

To establish the impact of the competition policy on prices, we calculated an index of prices in Canada relative to the U.S. for 1976, using the same methods we used in calculating the 1968 index. With all drugs equally weighted, the 1976 Canadian prices were 106.6 per cent of the U.S. prices, down slightly from the 110.1 per cent in 1968. The price index, with each drug weighted by quantity sold, was 93.6 per cent for 1976, practically the same as the 94.0 per cent in 1968. In other words, prices in Canada relative to the U.S. were essentially unchanged over the years 1968 to 1976.

These aggregate figures, however, tend to hide important information. Table 4-3 shows a breakdown of our drug sample into several categories. We see that both the equal- and quantity-weighted indices for drugs under compulsory license fell sharply between 1968 and 1976. Price reductions took place for seventeen of the twenty-three drugs in the subsample, and some of the decreases were surprisingly large. For example: 5 mg. tablets of diazepam (Valium) fell from 74.3 per cent of the U.S. price in 1968 to 6.1 per cent in 1976; 10 mg. tablets of chlordiazepoxide (Librium) fell from 80 to 35 per cent; and a 100 mg. injectable of hydrocortisone sodium succinate fell from 568 to 188 per cent. The two tranquilizers, Valium and Librium, represented a substantial share of the entire drug market, and their quantities weighed quite heavily on the final figures.

The drugs under compulsory license in 1976 represented 40 per cent of the sample's market value, and the price behaviour of the other 60 per cent of the sample was quite different. The patented, but not licensed, group experienced little overall change in price, although its index based on equal weight showed a substantial increase. The latter was probably due to new products being introduced at relatively high prices but selling in small volume. As for the other two categories, patent expired and remaining drugs, the former included drugs that were under patent in 1968 but not in 1976, and the latter included drugs that were not under patent in 1968, over-the-counter drugs, and others. Both of these categories experienced sharp price increases between 1968 and 1976, perhaps because they included mature products for which the influence of generic competition on prices was well

TABLE 4-3
1968 AND 1976 INDICES OF DRUG PRICES IN CANADA RELATIVE TO THE U.S., WITH THE SAMPLE CLASSIFIED BY THE PATENT STATUS OF THE DRUG IN 1976

	1968	*1976*
Under Compulsory License		
Price index based on equal weight	1.094	.792
Price index based on quantity weight	.933	.740
Percentage of total sample (weighted by market value)	38%	40%
Number of drugs in subsample	23	27
Patented, But Not Licensed		
Price index based on equal weight	.912	1.190
Price index based on quantity weight	.976	.937
Percentage of total sample (weighted by market value)	2%	10%
Number of drugs in subsample	7	11
Patent Expired		
Price index based on equal weight	.836	1.041
Price index based on quantity weight	.539	.717
Percentage of total sample (weighted by market value)	9%	4%
Number of drugs in subsample	9	11
Remaining Drugs		
Price index based on equal weight	1.131	1.109
Price index based on quantity weight	1.010	1.120
Percentage of total sample (weighted by market value)	51%	46%
Number of drugs in subsample	128	148
Total Sample		
Price index based on equal weight	1.101	1.066
Price index based on quantity weight	.940	.936
Percentage of total sample (weighted by market value)	100%	100%
Number of drugs in total sample	167	196

Source: See Appendix.

established by 1968. Also relevant was the fact that generic producers endeavour to establish brand names that, if successful, might allow them to raise their prices closer to those of the original producers.

A comparison of the prices of selected drugs in the U.S. and Canada by the RTPC found that U.S. prices were lower for a majority of the drugs, but no attempt was made to aggregate the data. A study by the Department of National Health and Welfare[4] showed that in 1970 Canadians paid on average 2 per cent more than Americans for an *unweighted* basket of selected tranquilizers, antibiotics, a heart drug, a sedative, an antidiabetic drug, and an antihistamine. However, our study clearly shows that the relative prices are sensitive to the sample selection and to the weighting system used.

Two other studies concentrated on the compulsory licensing issue. Fulda and Dickens[5] compared Canadian and American price changes between 1970 and 1974 for one dosage each of a sample of sixteen drugs that were under compulsory license. They found that Canadian prices (equally weighted) fell on average from 77.6 per cent of the U.S. prices in 1970 to 47.4 per cent in 1974. With each drug quantity-weighted, the decline was somewhat greater. Their results are more dramatic than those presented here, perhaps because they used a more restricted sample and a shorter time period. Gorecki and Klymchuk[6] also examined the effect of government intervention in the drug market and confirmed that compulsory licensing plus product selection have reduced drug prices at the manufacturers' level. They went on to demonstrate, though, that the savings were largely captured by the dispensing pharmacist—not passed on to the consumer.

The studies cited are consistent with our results in Table 4-3 for drugs under compulsory license. These studies, however, neither confirm nor contradict our finding that for all drugs the price level in Canada relative to the U.S. was unchanged between 1968 and 1976. Some evidence on this question may be obtained by using the change in the American and the Canadian price indices that are published for Canada and the U.S. by Statistics Canada and the U.S. Department of Labor Statistics, respectively, to arrive at a Canada-U.S. index for 1976. Letting $\hat{I}_{76}$ represent this 1976 "government" index, we computed it as follows:

$$\hat{I}_{76} = I_{68} \ \frac{II^c_{76}/II^c_{68}}{II^u_{76}/II^u_{68}}$$

where I_{68} is the Canada-U.S. price index from Table 4-3, and where II is the published government price index for each country, with the subscript denoting the year and the superscript denoting the country.

Based on the above, our estimate of the government index, $\hat{I}_{76}$, is .857, which is somewhat lower than the .933 we obtained from our price and volume data. This would suggest that Canadian prices in 1976 were lower relative to U.S. prices than indicated by Table 4-3. There are two reasons that could account for this difference, of which only one supports that conclusion. First, the government price indices include sales to hospitals as well as to pharmacies, whereas our Table 4-3 includes only the latter. It is possible that hospitals take advantage of generic substitutes to a greater degree than do pharmacies, in which case the prices paid by hospitals would fall more sharply. For instance, during the mid-Seventies, Hoffman–La Roche was virtually giving away tranquilizers (particularly Valium) to hospitals in order to prevent the generic producers from gaining a foothold.[7] Valium had a substantial sales volume that could have affected the 1976 government index significantly. Secondly, the Canadian government index is based on drugs produced in Canada, thereby effectively ignoring imports and goods resold by the pharmaceutical manufacturers, which typically are newer and, therefore, higher priced in Canada than in the U.S. The exclusion of hospitals from our index biases it upward, while the exclusion of imports from the government index biases it downward, so that the true fall in Canadian prices relative to U.S. prices is probably somewhere between the two numbers. With this qualification, we now see that the government index supports the accuracy of our index.[8]

What conclusions may we draw from the data in Table 4-3 on the impact of the government's competition policy on Canadian drug prices? The large fall in Canadian prices relative to the U.S. *on drugs for which compulsory licenses were obtained* suggests that the policy has been a huge success. This conclusion is tempered, however, by the rise in the prices of other drugs and by the modest fall in the price index for all drugs. This was due to a number of factors. At least two of these are outside the scope of the competition policy: (1) the index for all drugs includes over-the-counter drugs, which are not subject to the competition policy; and (2) between 1968 and 1976 wage rates rose more rapidly in Canada than in the U.S., causing prices in Canada to rise relative to the U.S. *on drugs not under compulsory license.* However, the relative rise in the prices of these latter drugs may also have been due in part to the competition policy and to the way in which it was being administered. That possibility and the future impact on

71

prices of the competition policy will be examined in chapter 5.

Expenditure Performance: Production Costs

Table 4-4 presents the condensed income statements for the Canadian and American drug industries for 1976 and the comparable percentage figures for 1968 from Table 3-1. We see that in both countries production cost as a percentage of the sales dollar increased—in Canada from 47.0 to 53.6 per cent, and in the U.S. from 33.0 to 38.8 per cent. The increase was somewhat larger for Canada, so that the difference in production cost as a percentage of sales between the two countries increased from 14.0 per cent in 1968 to 14.8 per cent in 1976. The reasons for these developments are examined below.

TABLE 4-4
CONDENSED INCOME STATEMENTS FOR THE CANADIAN AND U.S. DRUG INDUSTRIES, 1976
(millions of $'s)

	Canadian			U.S.		
	1976	1976	1968	1976	1976	1968
	($)	(%)	(%)	($)	(%)	(%)
Sales	865.7	100.0	100.0	13,016	100.0	100.0
Production costs:						
Material	383.1	44.3	39.1	3,813	29.3	23.5
Fuel and electricity	7.0	.8	.5	181	1.4	.7
Labour	74.0	8.5	7.4	1,053	8.1	8.8
Total	464.1	53.6	47.0	5,047	38.8	33.0
Gross profit	401.6	46.4	53.0	7,969	61.2	67.0

Source: See Appendix.

Material Cost

Table 4-5 classifies the sales and the costs according to whether the sales are resales or products of own manufacture. Panel A of Table 4-5 reveals that resales increased from 2.4 to 3.3 per cent of sales in the U.S., while they almost doubled from 11.6 to 19.3 per cent of sales in Canada. Resale products consist predominantly of imports of finished products from either multinational corporations abroad or from their subsidiaries in third countries; there is no manufacturing activity in Canada on these products. There is, of course, no technology transfer on resale products, and their increase from just over 10 per cent to just under 20 per cent of sales is a large step backward in technology transfer to Canadian subsidiaries from their parents abroad and in expenditure performance.

Panel B of Table 4-5 shows that while the cost of resale products was substantially unchanged for the U.S., the cost fell in Canada from 82.5 to 73.4 per cent of sales. Although this change was in the right direction, the latter figure still does not cover the selling and other overhead costs incurred in Canada on these products, and therefore, the transfer prices on resale products provided no profit to be reported in Canada. A transfer price equal to 73.4 per cent of sales is more than twice the production cost in the U.S. on these products, providing the parent companies with substantial profits on resale products.

Panel C of Table 4-5 contains the income statements for products of own manufacture. Material costs as a percentage of sales rose in both countries, but the increase in the U.S. from 22.6 to 28.3 per cent was somewhat larger than the Canadian increase from 33.4 to 37.3 per cent. The increase in both countries may have been due in some measure to a more rapid increase in material prices than in product prices, as a result of the industry's general decline in profitability beginning in the late Sixties. The increase may also have been due to the transfer of considerable production from the U.S. to Puerto Rico.

In order to stimulate employment in Puerto Rico, the U.S. made tax exempt the profits on subsidiaries located there. During the late Sixties and early Seventies U.S. drug firms began taking advantage of this tax haven, and by 1978 a *Business Week* article reported that the U.S. government was considering closing this tax loophole for the drug industry, because many firms were using transfer pricing to report 50 per cent or more of their total profits in their Puerto Rican subsidiaries.[9]

Some idea of the use of Puerto Rico as a tax haven is provided by the *U.S. Economic Census of Outlying Areas for 1977*. The Puerto Rican drug industry had shipments of $1,350 million, cost of materials of $327 million, and compensation of *all* employees of $96.6 million. Consequently, if all other expenses were as much as $100 million, the Puerto Rican subsidiaries had a reported, tax-free profit of over $800 million. By comparison, the *entire* U.S. industry had a pretax profit on its U.S. operations in 1976 of only about $1,700 million. Furthermore,

TABLE 4-5
SALES AND CONDENSED INCOME STATEMENTS FOR THE CANADIAN AND U.S. DRUG INDUSTRIES, CLASSIFIED BY RESALE PRODUCTS AND PRODUCTS OF OWN MANUFACTURE, 1976
(millions of $'s)

	Canadian			U.S.		
	1976	1976	1968	1976	1976	1968
	($)	(%)	(%)	($)	(%)	(%)
A. Classification of Sales by Type of Product						
Resale products	166.9	19.3	11.6	425	3.3	2.4
Products of own manufacture	698.8	80.7	88.4	12,591	96.7	97.6
Total	865.7	100.0	100.0	13,016	100.0	100.0
B. Income Statement for Resale Products						
Sales	166.9	100.0	100.0	425	100.0	100.0
Cost of sales:						
Domestic material	9.6	5.8	—	47	11.1	7.4
Import material	112.9	67.6	82.5	207	48.7	50.8
Total	122.5	73.4	82.5	254	59.8	58.2
Gross profit	44.4	26.6	17.5	171	40.2	41.8

C. Income Statement for Products of Own Manufacture

	Canadian			U.S.		
	1976	1976	1968	1976	1976	1968
	($)	(%)	(%)	($)	(%)	(%)
Sales	698.8	100.0	100.0	12,591	100.0	100.0
Production costs:						
Material: drug imports	64.2	9.2	6.5	923	7.3	.4
other imports	35.0	5.0	5.0	—	—	—
domestic materials	161.4	23.1	21.9	2,636	21.0	22.2
Subtotal	260.6	37.3	33.4	3,559	28.3	22.6
Fuel and electricity	7.0	1.0	.6	181	1.4	.8
Labour	74.0	10.6	8.3	1,053	8.4	9.0
Total	341.6	48.9	42.3	4,793	38.1	32.4
Gross profit	357.2	51.1	57.7	7,798	61.9	67.6

Source: See Appendix.

75

the above census reported that 71 per cent of the Puerto Rican drug shipments were to the U.S., and only 27 per cent went to foreign countries. It seems reasonable to conclude that the rise in material costs for the U.S. between 1968 and 1976 was in no small part due to the transfer of production to Puerto Rico and the high transfer prices on shipments to U.S. parent firms from their Puerto Rican subsidiaries.

These subsidiaries were also used to supply the Canadian market. The rise in Canada's cost of drug imports from 6.5 to 9.2 per cent was due in large measure to the high transfer prices. The small difference between American and Canadian income tax rates in 1968 created only a modest incentive to transfer Canadian profits abroad. However, the large difference between the Canadian tax rate and the zero rate in Puerto Rico materially increased the incentive for using transfer prices to reduce profits in Canada. The impact of the move to Puerto Rico on employment, taxes paid, and reported profits after taxes is discussed below.[10]

Labour Cost

In the U.S. the costs of production labour between 1968 and 1976 fell from 9.0 to 8.4 per cent of sales for products of own manufacture. This was largely a result of the transfer of production to Puerto Rico and the reduced labour content (or production per unit of output) in the U.S. In Canada production labour rose from 8.3 to 10.6 per cent of sales, due largely to the sharp rise in wage rates over the period. There is little evidence that the nature and scale of manufacturing activities changed.

Table 4-6 presents 1976 data analogous to the 1968 data in Table 3-3 on employment, compensation and output per worker in the two countries. The table reveals the sharp fall over the period in the ratio of the American wage rate to the Canadian. The 67 per cent excess of the American over the Canadian wage rate in 1968 had fallen to 22 per cent by 1976. To understand what took place in the drug industry, it should be realized that the American-Canadian spread in wage rates for most types of manufacturing jobs had been eliminated by 1976. Hence, the 22 per cent higher wage rate in the U.S. drug industry reflects either a higher skill content for the employment provided by the U.S. industry or the failure of wages in Canada to rise as rapidly in the drug industry as in other industries.

The narrowing of the wage differential between Canada and the U.S. could not have a favourable impact on employment in Canada, and the wage and tax incentives for production in Puerto Rico were

TABLE 4-6
EMPLOYMENT, COMPENSATION AND PRODUCTIVITY OF PRODUCTION WORKERS IN THE CANADIAN AND U.S. DRUG INDUSTRIES, 1976

	Canadian	U.S.		Ratio: U.S./Cdn	
				1976	1968
	(a)	(b)	(c)	(c/a)	(—)
Total production hours (000)	13,178	150,900		11.45	11.79
	(Cdn $)	(U.S. $)	(Cdn $)		
Total compensation of production workers (000)	74,016	1,053,200	1,038,700	14.03	19.43
Hourly compensation	5.62	6.98	6.88	1.22	1.68
Total value of output (000)	698,800	12,591,000	12,417,200	17.77	18.30
Value of output per production hour	53.03	83.44	82.29	1.55	1.55

Source: See Appendix.

77

unfavourable to both countries. In the U.S., production employment increased by only 15 per cent between 1968 and 1976, while the nominal value of sales increased by 131 per cent, and the real value of sales increased by 61 per cent. The large difference between the percentage increases in employment and sales was due partly to increased productivity, but it was also due to the transfer of production to Puerto Rico. In Canada the nominal and real value of sales rose during the period by 135 and 79 per cent, respectively, while production employment rose by only 19 per cent. It would appear that the same forces were at work on employment in Canada as in the U.S.

The Canadian market is served in part by subsidiaries of European manufacturers. While some of them may have found wage rates in Canada falling relative to their wage rates at home, they too were moving production to other countries, such as Ireland and Portugal, that offered much lower wage rates than Canada and also provided tax-free shelters for profits.

Expenditure Performance: Overhead Costs

Turning to Table 4-7, we see that some elements of overhead costs and profits changed little as a percentage of sales, while others changed materially. In aggregate, they fell in both countries, since some combination of a squeeze on margins and a transfer of profits to subsidiaries subject to low tax rates reduced gross profits. In the U.S., gross profits fell from 67.0 to 61.2 per cent of sales, while in Canada they fell from 53.0 to 46.4 per cent of sales.

R&D expenditures rose from 7.5 to 9.2 per cent of sales in the U.S., perhaps because of the stricter standards for the approval of new products that were adopted. However, in Canada expenditures remained at 3.0 per cent of sales, meaning that in real terms R&D did not increase proportionately with sales, because salary rates for the persons employed in R&D undoubtedly matched the sharp rise in Canadian pay scales between 1968 and 1976. One explanation is, undoubtedly, that the drug industry was highly upset with the competition policy adopted by the government, and it responded by holding down R&D expenditures. Industry representatives had made a number of announcements over the years to the effect that programs to expand R&D in Canada were not adopted in response to the competition policy.[11] The maintenance of expenditures at 3 per cent of sales in the face of this hostility may be all that one could hope for.

Compensation of salaried employees other than those in R&D fell slightly as a percentage of sales in both countries, but the percentage

TABLE 4-7
DISTRIBUTION OF GROSS PROFITS FOR THE CANADIAN AND U.S. DRUG INDUSTRIES, 1976
(millions of $'s)

	Canadian			U.S.		
	Dollar Amount	Per cent of Sales		Dollar Amount	Per cent of Sales	
	1976	1976	1968	1976	1976	1968
Gross profit	401.6	46.4	53.0	7,969	61.2	67.0
Overhead costs:						
Cost of research and development:						
Payroll	14.0	1.6	1.8	729	5.6	4.5
Purchased services	11.9	1.4	1.2	472	3.6	3.0
Subtotal	25.9	3.0	3.0	1,201	9.2	7.5
Salary compensation other than R&D	120.9	14.0	14.9	1,346	10.3	10.5
Non-payroll selling expenses:						
Travel and entertainment	41.9	4.8	7.1	526	4.0	2.1
Advertising and promotion	45.1	5.2	7.5	1,296	10.0	10.1
Subtotal	87.0	10.0	14.6	1,822	14.0	12.2
Purchased business services	39.7	4.6	4.7	943	7.3	4.0
Depreciation expense	14.7	1.7	1.7	316	2.4	2.1
Other overhead costs	59.9	6.9	6.8	693	5.3	6.5
Total overhead costs	348.1	40.2	45.7	6,321	48.5	42.8
Income taxes	24.1	2.8	3.7	593	4.6	10.9
Net profit after taxes	29.4	3.4	3.6	1,055	8.1	13.3

Source: See Appendix.

remained substantially higher for Canada—14.0 per cent versus 10.3 per cent for the U.S. More interesting is what happened to the number and compensation of such employees in the two countries. Table 4-8 reveals that American/Canadian ratio for the number of salaried employees rose sharply from 9.62 to 12.04 between 1968 and 1976. What took place was a 35.9 per cent increase in the number of salaried employees in the U.S. and a much smaller, 8.6 per cent, increase in Canada. By contrast, compensation per employee rose more rapidly in Canada, so that the American/Canadian ratio fell from 1.58 to 1.26. Compensation per employee more than doubled in Canada and increased by 61 per cent in the U.S.

The much smaller increase in salaried employment in Canada than in the U.S. was due to a number of factors. One was the continued reduction in selling activity toward a more reasonable level, due in part perhaps to the government's competition policy, which made selling activity less profitable. Secondly, the substantial rise in the compensation rates in Canada undoubtedly stimulated a more rational and efficient use of management personnel. This rationalization of management functions may also have benefited from the "settling down" of organizations that followed the acquisitions and entry of new firms during the Sixties. It is also possible that management responsibilities were being centralized in response to the progress in information processing and communication that was taking place. Finally, the management responsibilities of the Canadian subsidiaries may have been contracted in retaliation against the competition policy. There certainly is no evidence that the responsibilities of Canadian subsidiaries were enlarged between 1968 and 1976.

The more rapid increase in the compensation rate for salaried persons in Canada between 1968 and 1976 was due primarily, if not exclusively, to the general rise in pay scales in Canada relative to the U.S. However, average salary per employee in 1976 was still 26 per cent higher in the U.S., and there is no evidence that the qualitative level of the employment opportunities in Canada moved closer to the U.S. level.

Returning to Table 4-7, we see that selling expenses other than employee compensation rose slightly as a percentage of sales in the U.S., and they fell sharply from 14.6 to 10.0 per cent of sales in Canada. The latter reflects the continuing reduction in the scale of selling activity that was mentioned above.

In the U.S. between 1968 and 1976, purchased business services increased sharply as a percentage of sales from 4.0 to 7.3 per cent,

TABLE 4-8
EMPLOYMENT, COMPENSATION AND SALES PER EMPLOYEE FOR SALARIED EMPLOYEES IN THE CANADIAN AND U.S. DRUG INDUSTRIES, 1976

	Canadian	U.S.		Ratio: U.S./Cdn	
				1976	1968
	(a)	(b)	(c)	(c/a)	(—)
Number of salaried employees	7,958	95,800		12.04	9.62
	(Cdn $)	(U.S. $)	(Cdn $)		
Total compensation of salaried employees (000)	134,905	2,075,500	2,046,351	15.17	15.24
Average compensation	16,954	21,665	21,361	1.26	1.58
Total sales (000)	865,700	13,016,000	12,836,000	14.83	16.56
Sales per salaried employee	108,783	135,866	133,991	1.23	1.72

Source: See Appendix.

81

while other overhead costs fell from 6.5 to 5.3 per cent. In Canada both remained about the same percentage of sales, suggesting again (in view of the higher increase in compensation rates in Canada) that any movements in management responsibilities that did take place in Canada were out of—not into—the country. Finally, there was no material change in depreciation expense as a percentage of sales in either country.

The consequence of the above developments was that all overhead costs rose from 42.8 to 48.5 per cent of sales in the U.S., while in Canada the percentages fell from 45.7 to 40.2 per cent. The increase in the U.S. was due to the increase in R&D, sales promotion, and other overhead expenditures in order to maintain gross-profit margins and increase market share in the face of increased competition and a decline in important new product innovations. During this period European and American firms became more aggressive in each other's home markets. In Canada, sales expenditures fell in response to the government's competition policy, which made such expenditures less profitable, and in response to the criticisms of their previous high levels.[12]

Profit and Income Tax Performance

Net profit before taxes fell in the U.S. from 24.2 per cent to 12.7 per cent of sales from 1968 to 1976, with the transfer of reported profits to Puerto Rico and the rise in overhead costs being the two main reasons for such a drastic fall. Income tax expense fell sharply from 10.9 to 4.6 per cent of sales, due to changes in the effective tax rate that were instituted for the stated purpose of stimulating investment in the U.S. Consequently, net profit after taxes fell by almost one-half, from 13.3 to 8.1 per cent.

Since reported net profit before taxes in Canada was only 7.3 per cent of sales in 1968, there was very little room for their further reduction in 1976. Nonetheless, they fell to 6.2 per cent. Favourable changes in the Canadian tax law made the income tax fall more sharply than net profit after taxes. The former fell from 3.7 to 2.8 per cent of sales, while the after-tax net profit fell from 3.6 to 3.4 per cent of sales. As explained in chapter 3, the pretax net profit grossly understates the contribution of Canadian subsidiaries to their foreign parents.

Conclusion: Technology Transfer

Recall that the term "technology transfer" can be defined to mean

TABLE 4-9
ALLOCATION OF REVENUES FROM THE CANADIAN DRUG INDUSTRY BETWEEN CANADIAN AND FOREIGN RECIPIENTS, 1976
(thousands of $'s)

	Canadian Recipients		Foreign Recipients	
	(Cdn $)	*(%)*	*(Cdn $)*	*(%)*
Material cost	171.0	19.8	198.2	22.9
Import tariff	13.9	1.6		
Fuel and electricity	7.0	0.8		
Production labour	74.0	8.5		
Cost of research and development	24.8	2.9	1.1	0.1
Salary compensation other than R&D	120.9	14.0		
Non-payroll selling expenses	87.0	10.0		
Purchased business services	16.9	2.0	22.8	2.6
Depreciation expense	14.7	1.7		
Other overhead costs	59.9	6.9		
Income taxes	24.1	2.8		
Net profit after taxes	0.3	0.0	29.1	3.4
Total	614.5	71.0	251.2	29.0

Source: See Appendix.

either of two things. One is *transfer to* another country of the parent firm's production expertise, and the other is *replication in* that country of the parent firm's level and quality of expenditures. On the first definition, there is no evidence that production methods in Canada's drug industry were upgraded as a result of the transfer of technology from abroad. Undoubtedly, the secondary manufacture of some new products was introduced into Canada through instructions on how to compound each new product, but that can hardly be considered a technology transfer of any significance.

On the level and quality of expenditures in Canada, Table 4-9 presents the 1976 allocation of revenues from the Canadian drug industry between Canadian and foreign recipients. Expenditures abroad increased from 25.3 per cent of sales revenue in 1968 (Table 3-7) to 29.0 per cent in 1976. The scenario that multinational corporations are *supposed* to follow is first to enter a foreign country through exports into it and then to replace these exports, as time passes and volume expands, with domestic production and supporting activities. This standard scenario was reversed between 1968 and 1976: imports rose from 17.8 to 22.9 per cent of the sales dollar. The only bright spot in Table 4-9 is the near elimination of expenditures abroad by Canadian subsidiaries for R&D.

However, the above figures understate the curtailment of activity in Canada between 1968 and 1976. As shown earlier in this chapter, the sharp rise in wage and salary rates in Canada in relation to the U.S. and in relation to drug prices, masked the sharp fall in Canadian employment in relation to sales. Either the productivity of management and professional employees in Canada increased sharply without an increase in their responsibilities, or the activities they performed were transferred out of Canada. The analysis carried out earlier supports the latter hypothesis. In view of the widely stated policy of the multinationals to withdraw expenditures—not sales revenue—from Canada, the failure of expenditures in Canada to fall even more in relation to sales revenue may be considered fortunate.

Policy Options and Recommendations

5

In the theoretical literature, certainly in the polemic literature, on the problem of formulating an industrial strategy, we find the extreme solutions of complete free enterprise on the one hand and complete regulation on the other, with the latter often including the prohibition of foreign ownership—or even including the adoption of government ownership. Depending on what is assumed about the nature of the human and institutional environment in which industry functions, either of these solutions can be shown to be the optimal industrial strategy. Unfortunately, however, the real world does not satisfy any of the strong assumptions required. It is not surprising, therefore, to find that government policy in Canada falls somewhere on middle ground.

Our study of the Canadian pharmaceutical industry has reinforced our belief that simple polar solutions to economic problems are neither feasible nor desirable. Rather, our investigation made clear that the viable options open to the Canadian government are:

- a continuation of present policies;
- various departures from present policies in the direction of reduced government intervention;
- various departures from present policies in the direction of greater government intervention.

Building on our earlier chapters, this final chapter will identify and evaluate the various components of these three policy options for the pharmaceutical industry. In addition, policies to reduce foreign ownership will be investigated.

Present Policies

The major elements of present government policies for the pharmaceutical industry are:

- the modest encouragement of domestic production through a low tariff on the import of any drug for which a substitute is being produced in Canada;
- the protection of consumer health through the testing of new drugs and the inspection of manufacturing facilities;
- the encouragement of price competition through the compulsory licensing of patented drugs and the authorization of product selection (substitution) by the pharmacist.

What results can we expect in Canada from these policies—for drug prices, for production, for R&D and other activities?

Drug Prices

Over the last two decades, the primary objective of government policies for the pharmaceutical industry has been the encouragement of competition in order to reduce drug prices. For this purpose, bold legislation has been passed that allows generic producers to obtain compulsory licenses on patented prescription drugs and that allows the pharmacist to substitute a generic product for the brand-name drug prescribed by the doctor. As we saw in chapter 4, this legislation has resulted in dramatically reduced list prices for certain drugs. However, the overall impact of the government's competition policy has been far less beneficial and in the future may be even less so as manufacturers adapt their marketing strategies to this regulatory environment.

The prices of drug products for which compulsory licensing had provided generic substitutes by 1976 fell from 93 per cent of their U.S. prices in 1968 to 74 per cent in 1976. However, on *all* drugs, prices in Canada did not fall materially relative to the U.S. As stated in chapter 4, this was due in large measure to factors outside the scope of the competition policy—to inclusion in the total sample of over-the-counter drugs and to the rise in Canadian wage rates relative to those in the U.S. However, this modest performance of the overall price index was also due to the small number of drugs for which compulsory licensing created generic substitutes by 1976—only twenty-seven. Furthermore, it is possible that the rise in prices for drugs without generic substitutes was motivated in part by the manufacturers' desire to recover profits lost on products subject to generic competition and by their judgment that price policy need no longer be influenced by the objective of avoiding hostile government legislation.

The suggestion that strategic objectives and a satisfactory level of profits could influence the prices charged by a firm is considered heresy by some economists, who maintain that all firms maximize profits. Profit maximization may be true of firms in a competitive industry, but in such an industry each firm has no control over its prices. In the drug industry each firm has considerable latitude in setting its prices, and there is general agreement that it does so with the objective of earning a satisfactory return on capital after covering a level of R&D, selling and other expenditures necessary to ensure the long-run prosperity of the firm. A "selfish" motive for such a policy is the recognition that the goodwill of government is an important factor in a firm's long-run success. Insofar as the firms in the industry price in this way, the price reductions on drugs subject to compulsory licensing would be offset by higher prices on other products.

More disturbing than the rise in price of those products with no generic substitutes is the small number of products for which there are substitutes available. The passage of time is not likely to change this state of affairs. Generic producers find it profitable to compete on only a few high-volume products, since the marketing strategies for a product (to be described shortly) that are pursued by the brand-name producers confine the generics to a small share of the product's market.[1] Obviously, a small share of the market on a small-volume product imposes costs on the generic producer that make it very difficult to compete with the brand-name producer.

It may be instructive to consider why the cost disadvantage to the generic producer is prohibitive, notwithstanding the high gross-profit margin that the brand-name producer enjoys. First, the investment in time and money required to bring a new product on the market is substantial—even for a generic producer—and is independent of sales. Secondly, the unit production costs are very high for a product that represents only a small fraction of a small market. By comparison, the brand-name producers are vertically integrated and import their finished products, making their unit production costs (based on worldwide sales) much lower. Finally, the distribution costs are to some degree independent of sales volume, and they are spread over a larger output for the brand-name producer. For these reasons, generic competition will probably remain confined to a few large-volume products.

On those products subject to generic competition, the marketing strategies of the brand-name producers will likely continue in the future to reduce the extent of price competition. Their cardinal principle is to avoid price competition, and they are quite resourceful in discovering strategies that realize this goal. One such strategy is the replacement of price competition with "discount" competition. It may be described as follows. Assume that the Parcost price of a brand-name pill is 10¢ and that a generic producer comes on the market with a substitute for 3¢. At first glance, one might think that the price of the brand-name pill would fall—if not to 3¢, then to a slight premium over that price. However, it does not work that way. On prescriptions paid for by the *province*, the price would be 3¢, but on prescriptions paid for by the *consumer*, the brand-name product would remain (as we saw in Table 4-2) at 10¢. The pharmacist may dispense the brand-name product (assuming the doctor prescribed it) and charge 10¢ per pill plus the prescription fee. Other things the same, the pharmacist might be expected to make the substitution and charge the customer only 3¢ per pill. However, other things are not the same. The brand-name firm offers the pharmacist a volume discount so that the actual cost of its pill is only 8¢, which gives the pharmacist a profit of 2¢ over and above the prescription fee when dispensing the brand-name pill on prescriptions paid for by the customer.[2] Even more detrimental to the generic producer, the volume discount may be so structured that the pharmacist finds it more profitable to dispense the brand-name product on *provincially* paid prescriptions as well and not to stock the generic product at all.

This discount strategy of brand-name producers influences the behaviour of the generic producers, who are motivated to price future generic substitutes only slightly below the prices of the brand-name products and to compete with quantity discounts instead of with price. However, they are at a disadvantage in this form of competition, since the discount that a firm can offer varies with its list price. Nonetheless, discounting becomes the form of competition that generic firms are compelled to adopt.

It is our conclusion that the government's present competition policy can be expected to reduce drug prices less in the future than in the past. We have seen that generic producers will not enter the market for the numerous low-volume products that represent about 80 per cent of total sales, and that the prices of these products may even be pushed up by the competition policy. On the few large-volume products, generic producers will reduce their list prices less in the future than in the past, because quantity discounts are replacing reductions in list prices as a means of competition. Furthermore, the quantity discounts they can offer will be moderated by the rise in their costs due to the inefficiencies of having the production and the distribution of high-volume products (economies of scale are very important in marketing) shared by a large number of firms.

Finally, the quantity-discount route to price reductions does not benefit the ultimate consumers, since the resulting rise in the list prices of generic products reduces the benefits of the government's competiton policy on prescriptions paid for by the province, and since the pharmacist does not pass on to the consumer the quantity discount he receives.

Production

As stated previously, a widely held view of the multinational corporation is that it first enters a foreign country through exports, and then—with the passage of time and with its increased sales in and knowledge of the country—it introduces and expands production in the country. This pattern of development, however, was reversed for the Canadian drug industry during the period from 1968 to 1976, when the fraction of the Canadian market served by imports originating from parent countries or other subsidiaries abroad increased, while the fraction of the market served by Canadian subsidiaries fell.

This substitution of imports for domestic production continued at an accelerated rate from 1976 to 1979 (the last year for which data could be obtained), as shown in Table 5-1 on page 90.

We see that in the eight years from 1968 to 1976 net imports rose from 13.9 to 19.3 per cent of sales, and in only three more years they rose further to 26.3 per cent. Over the same two time spans, net exports rose much less rapidly, so that the trade deficit as a percentage of sales rose from 9.7 to 14.2 to 20.1.

The large increase in drug imports into Canada may have been due in part to the government's competition policy, which the multinational drug firms viewed as an expression of hostility, making them less inclined to follow policies designed to secure the government's goodwill. However, other developments during the period may have actually played a larger role in the transfer of production abroad. Prior to the mid-Sixties, a multinational's alternative to producing in Canada was producing in its home plant in the U.S., England, Germany or the like. The comparative advantage of producing in its home plant was relatively small and declining, certainly for high-volume drug products, while the various advantages (especially goodwill) of

TABLE 5-1
FOREIGN TRADE STATISTICS FOR DRUG PRODUCTS

	1968		1976		1979*	
	($)	(%)	($)	(%)	($)	(%)
Sales	368,511,000	100.0	865,595,000	100.0	1,085,000,000	100.0
Net imports	51,272,000	13.9	166,704,000	19.3	285,538,000	26.3
Net exports	15,350,000	4.2	43,975,000	5.1	67,849,000	6.3
Trade deficit	35,922,000	9.7	122,729,000	14.2	217,689,000	20.1

* The sales figure for 1979 is our estimate.

Source: Statistics Canada, *Trade of Canada: Imports, Merchandise Trade* (Ottawa: various years).

producing in Canada were considerable and led to the gradual growth of production over time. However, after the mid-Sixties, the much lower production costs and the considerable tax advantages of producing in Puerto Rico, Ireland, Portugal or similar places, persuaded the multinational drug firms to begin transferring production to these countries. The advantages were even substantial when compared to production at home. The initial transfers were on an experimental basis, but as experience increased and as the benefits became obvious, transfers to these low-wage, low-tax havens increased—not only from the high-cost Canadian subsidiaries but also from the lower-cost plants at home.

For Canada, importing fine chemicals had been the rule, but what took place during the Seventies was the massive transfer abroad of the secondary stages of drug manufacture, including the production of the end product. In addition to the substantially lower wage and tax rates in countries such as Puerto Rico, a reduction in the Canadian tariff on taxable imports from 15 to 10 per cent contributed to this trend. A further impetus during the Seventies was the squeeze on profit margins caused, among other things, by the increasing cost of testing new products and the decreasing return on R&D—as the "easy" discoveries of new drugs were exhausted.

Exemption from the corporation income tax was probably the single most important consideration in moving production abroad to places such as Puerto Rico.[3] It may be thought that such transfer of secondary manufacturing abroad is not needed to enjoy a tax advantage. Superficially, that could be achieved simply by raising the transfer price for fine chemicals to a level that would leave no profit in Canada. However, tax authorities do on occasion look at transfer prices, and the transfer of profits abroad that can be justified to the tax authorities increases with the production transferred abroad. Furthermore, the tax-haven countries expect production employment as a quid pro quo for their generous tax concessions, and their goodwill is of concern to the multinational drug companies.

The above considerations lead us to believe that the continuation of present government policies—tariff and competition—will result in the further transfer of drug production abroad and a rise in imports to possibly 35 or even 40 per cent of sales by 1985. Since the cost of imports is only a fraction of their sales value, the extent to which drugs will be produced abroad will be much higher than 35 per cent. If the cost of imports averages 50 per cent of their sales value, imports equal to 35 per cent of sales imply that 70 per cent of production is taking place abroad.

Overhead Activities

In the drug industry, production costs are small relative to overhead costs. Therefore, the consequences of maintaining current policies for the location of overhead activities in Canada are of considerable interest. This is particularly true of R&D, which is considered to be of such great benefit to society-at-large that it is frequently subsidized by government. Unfortunately, R&D appears to be the area that has suffered the most from the government's competition policy. Corporations that engage in the R&D and sales promotion required to discover and sell new drugs believe quite naturally that their large gross-profit margins are absolutely necessary to recover their costs. Therefore, they view the objective of the competition policy as a threat to their very existence, and they consider the withdrawal of R&D activity from Canada as a legitimate response to that policy.

We saw in chapter 4 that the industry's R&D expenditure was about the same percentage of sales in 1976 as it was in 1968. However, in real terms R&D fell in relation to sales, and there is more or less firm evidence that increased R&D activity in Canada—that would otherwise have been undertaken—was not carried out.[4] Canada's attractiveness for expanding R&D expenditures is discussed further in the next section.

The various components of selling expenses represent a large fraction of overhead costs. These costs fell between 1968 and 1976 because they were widely acknowledged to be excessive in 1968. They may continue to fall because the economic environment created by the competition policy reduces the usefulness of sales promotion. However, the competition policy does not lead to the transfer abroad of sales activity, because that activity must be carried out in the country where the sales occur.

In addition to R&D and selling, other overhead activities are undertaken to serve them and production as well, and consequently, they are incurred here or abroad to the extent that these primary activities are located here or abroad.[5] Hence, as R&D, selling and production activities decline in Canada under present policies, we can expect expenditures in Canada for supporting overhead activities to decline as a percentage of sales.

The final distributive share of the sales dollar is profits before taxes. Profits *net of the corporate income tax* that are earned by Canadian subsidiaries may be recognized in their accounts and then transferred abroad, or they may be transferred abroad by means of transfer prices and service charges. Which course of action the multinationals follow is of no consequence to Canada, but *reported profits before taxes* are of interest because they determine taxes paid *to* Canada. Unfortunately, the various tax havens abroad that are available to multinational corporations provide a powerful incentive to minimize reported profits in Canada, and the reduction of economic activity in Canada under present policies further reduces reported profits here, since the two are correlated.

Less Interventionist Policies

The areas in which governments might adopt less interventionist policies are the tariff, approval of new drugs, and compulsory licensing. However, only the last holds any hope for improving industry performance.

Tariff and Approval of New Drugs

The tariff no longer has any influence on the mix between imports and production in Canada. In 1976 imports that were free of duty comprised 38.5 per cent of all imports, and the duty on the remainder was only 10.1 per cent, down sharply from the 15.2 per cent in 1968. With production cost a small fraction of sales price and with the duty already so low, a further reduction—even to the point of complete elimination—would go practically unnoticed.

As for new drugs, the least interventionist policy that government could follow in controlling their introduction and the conditions of their manufacture would be to eliminate controls altogether. However, this would be more likely to reduce than to increase R&D expenditures in Canada, and it would not likely have any influence on other expenditures. Concern for human health will undoubtedly rule out the elimination of controls. A more realistic alternative in the direction of less intervention would be to approve for use in Canada any drug that had obtained approval in another country considered to have adequate control standards.[6] This would reduce R&D expenditures in Canada, and it would reduce the governmental cost of evaluating test results. It is open to question whether or not the government's present policy of evaluating for itself each new drug, even though reliably approved for use elsewhere, is worth the resultant cost and delay. However, even if secondary testing in Canada were to provide no health benefits, its elimination would benefit the country only if the cost saving were passed on to consumers in some way—for example, through lower prices. Otherwise, such testing provides an employment benefit—even though a ''featherbedding'' one.

93

Compulsory Licensing

The areas in which the industry is most anxious to see a reduction in government intervention is in compulsory licensing and product selection. Actually, the elimination of either would be adequate, since one without the other would have little influence, but for several reasons the Pharmaceutical Manufacturers Association of Canada (PMAC) has been more concerned with compulsory licensing. First and foremost, having to grant a license at a nominal royalty on a product that required a fortune to develop is considered to be most unfair. Secondly, compulsory licensing is a federal law, and only one government need be persuaded to eliminate it. Finally, it would be most difficult to persuade those provinces that have authorized product selection to reverse themselves, since their primary interest in the drug industry is the prices charged to themselves or to their residents.

The industry would like to have compulsory licensing completely eliminated or, short of that, to have a reasonable period legislated between the introduction of a new drug and the granting of a compulsory license. The position of the PMAC is that a favourable change in the law would result in a marked expansion of R&D activity in Canada, and it is likely that some expansion would take place. In addition, there are some objective factors that support this conclusion. Without doubt, the human, medical and educational resources, and the other attributes of our socio-economic environment, make it possible to carry on a higher level of R&D in Canada. Furthermore, we understand that the compensation rates for scientists and doctors in Canada compare very favourably with compensation rates in the U.S. and Europe, making it possible to do the same work here at a lower cost than abroad.[7]

There are reasons to believe, however, that the rate of growth in the industry's R&D expenditures in Canada would be modest. Human testing requires doctors trained in a specialized branch of pharmacology. Their supply cannot be increased very rapidly—and then only with the cooperation of the medical schools and probably with the financial support of government. Although the supply of chemists and other scientists who develop new products is undoubtedly more flexible, creative research organizations cannot be established overnight. Finally, while multinational corporations are not oblivious to the countries in which their major markets are located, powerful forces are at work to maintain and expand the existing research organizations that are located "at home."

What are the reasons for not reaching an accommodation with the industry on compulsory licensing? Our previous discussion of the impact of competition policy on product prices suggests that the loss there in terms of higher prices is not likely to be great. But the elimination of compulsory licensing would be a severe blow to the generic producers, a significant fraction of which are domestically owned, whereas the nongeneric producers are practically all owned abroad. The association of Canadian-owned pharmaceutical companies in the English-speaking provinces, which represents the views of the generic producers, opposes the elimination of compulsory licensing. It proposes instead that government incentives be provided for the expansion of R&D, production and other activities in Canada.[8]

Perhaps the major reason why the drug industry and the government were not able to reach a mutually satisfactory agreement on compulsory licensing was the broad strategic objectives of the foreign multinationals that control the PMAC. Lang wrote a very detailed history of the events leading up to the establishment of compulsory licensing. He was convinced (in part on the basis of information provided by a former director of the PMAC) that the primary concern of the industry was to avoid any precedent that might be followed in other countries,[9] making it unwilling to accept any change in the status quo. Now, the industry proposes that the legislation be amended to allow ten years from the date a drug is introduced into Canada before a license must be granted, and it predicts substantial benefits to Canada in terms of investment, employment, R&D and exports.[10]

Ten years of exclusive sale from the date the product is introduced would be quite generous, since the life of a patent from the date it is granted is only seventeen years. However, the proposal does suggest the possibility of reaching a reasonable accommodation with the industry, and we are persuaded that such an accommodation would be preferable to the present state of affairs. Now, a compulsory license can be obtained as soon as the patent is issued, but in practice the patent holder can expect to have at least five years free of generic competition, since a generic producer is unlikely to seek a license until it is clear that the sales in Canada will be adequate to justify generic competition. That will not be known until the original product has been on the Canadian market for three or four years, and then the generic producer will require another year or two to bring out its substitute. We recommend, therefore, a five-year period before a compulsory license must be granted, guaranteeing the original producer at least six years without generic competition, and an even longer period before effective competition could materialize.[11] Such legislation would seem to be a reasonable compromise, if the industry would make clear its commitment to increased R&D expenditures.

A final point to note on the subject of less interventionist policies pertains to the overlapping of federal and provincial regulation: this overlapping imposes costs on the industry that could be reduced if the two levels of regulation were integrated.

More Interventionist Policies

Greater intervention by government in the Canadian drug industry can take either of two broad directions. One direction embraces policies designed to reduce prices, or increase production, or increase other activities, with no explicit concern for how these policies might influence the mix of foreign and domestic ownership. The other direction involves the reduction of foreign ownership, either to achieve the above price and expenditure objectives or because domestic ownership is desired as an end in itself. Policies that are concerned directly with drug prices and with expenditures for production, R&D and income taxes are examined in this section, while intervention to reduce foreign ownership is taken up in the following section.

Drug Prices

We have seen that the impact of compulsory licensing and product selection on the overall level of drug prices, particularly at the consumer level, has been very modest. Furthermore, the benefits that have been achieved are likely to be eroded in the future as countervailing strategies by the industry take effect. The problems of securing price competition may be summarized as follows. Without both compulsory licensing and product selection, the doctor will decide the brand to be consumed, selecting a brand-name product without regard for price. The government's competition policy transfers the selection decision to the pharmacist, but the discount— and perhaps other marketing—strategies adopted by the brand-name producers make it more profitable for the pharmacist to select the higher-priced, brand-name product. This not only denies the consumer the lower price of the generic substitute, it also limits the range of drugs for which compulsory licenses are sought, because the generic producer cannot expect to make a satisfactory profit on low-volume products.

To eliminate ''discount competition'' and to restore the price competition intended by the legislation authorizing product selection, it would be required that the pharmacist pass on to the consumer the quantity discount received from the manufacturer. In short, the price to the consumer should be the prescription fee plus the actual cost to the pharmacist of the drug that is dispensed.[12] This change in the legislation would benefit the generic producer as well as the consumer. Note, however, that it requires action on the provincial, not the federal, level.

It would be desirable to go beyond the above measures and try to involve the consumer in the selection process. A modest step in this direction might be the conspicuous posting of Parcost-type data in every drug store on the various prices of each drug for which two or more brands are available. Perhaps a more effective course of action would be to give an organization such as the Consumers' Association of Canada a subsidy to publicize this price information so that persons who are concerned with the prices they pay for prescription drugs would have reasonable access to the information required for an intelligent choice. This consumer benefit should more than justify the cost of the subsidy.

It should be added, however, that the multinationals are also using methods other than discounting to restrict generic competition. They have initiated a number of lawsuits to prohibit generic producers from using pills of the same colour and size as the original product. In addition, they have asked the courts to restrict the scope of the legislation under which compulsory licenses are granted. Even if this legal action should ultimately fail, it certainly harasses the generic producers.

A radical means for reducing drug prices would be legislation that requires the pharmacist to charge the consumer the prescription fee plus the list price for the least expensive, approved drug. This, in essence, is what Saskatchewan does now.[13] Such legislation, however, could have consequences that are undesirable. For reasons that will be presented below in the section on foreign ownership, we do not recommend this course of action.

Production

Production in Canada can be increased through several means: a higher tariff, tax concessions, subsidies and quotas. However, all but the tariff can be discounted quite easily. Canada cannot compete in providing tax incentives, since numerous countries are offering complete exemption from taxes. There may be special circumstances surrounding a class of products that make it advisable to subsidize their production in Canada, but the characteristics of the industry do not justify direct subsidies as a matter of general policy. So-called voluntary quotas have been imposed on foreign suppliers by the U.S. to reconcile its desire to have trade barriers reduced throughout the world with its need to give "temporary" protection to certain industries at home. Apart from such political considerations, import quotas would seem to be inferior to the tariff as a means of encouraging domestic industry.

It is quite likely that a rise in the tariff on drugs from the present level of 10 per cent to a figure in the range of 20 to 25 per cent would be needed to reverse the substitution of imports for domestic production that has taken place since 1968. Such an increase would have a favourable influence on secondary drug manufacture, but primary manufacture (for example, fine chemicals) would only be encouraged for the small number of products for which economies of scale are not large and for which an export market is not required to absorb the output of an efficient operation.

The case for a higher tariff to increase production rests on the attractiveness of the pay scales, type of work, and other attributes of employment in the drug industry. Direct production employment is attractive, but perhaps more important is the employment of technical and other salaried persons in work related to the production process. The ratio of such indirect production employees to persons directly employed in the production process is exceptionally high in the drug industry.

Unfortunately, there are some strong reasons why the tariff on drugs should not be raised. First, Canada has agreed with the other industrial nations of the world through the General Agreement on Tariffs and Trade (GATT) to a long-run policy of tariff reductions. Hence, a rise in the tariff on drugs could only take place as part of a general change in Canada's tariff policy. Secondly, insofar as production in Canada is increased at the expense of less-developed countries (such as Ireland, Portugal and Puerto Rico) and not at the expense of the wealthy industrial powers, raising the tariff may be considered a rejection of Canada's international responsibilities to the less prosperous countries of the world. Finally, a rise in the tariff may in some measure raise prices to consumers.

Research and Development
We have seen that R&D in Canada may be increased, more or less, by reaching an accommodation with the multinational corporations on the

98

length of time during which the discoverer of a new drug may enjoy its exclusive production. A widely recommended alternative to this policy is the granting of government subsidies to industry for R&D activity—an alternative that we consider to be inadvisable for a number of reasons. First, it would not provide "spin-off" benefits in terms of employment in production or other activities, since the location of R&D is largely independent of the location of a firm's other activities. While the location of R&D in a multinational's home country might have spin-off benefits, this rarely occurs from stimulating R&D in a subsidiary country. Secondly, the task of identifying those corporations that can make good use of a government subsidy would be quite difficult. If preference were given to Canadian-owned companies, their small number and size would make it unlikely the money would be spent well, and such preference would give rise to political objections on the grounds that the program should not discriminate against "good corporate citizens," even though foreign-owned. On the other hand, failure to discriminate against foreign-owned corporations would also be politically objectionable. Finally, since subsidy programs often lack continuity, they tend to be wasteful. An effective R&D organization can only be developed slowly over time. Since there is a long period during which R&D's output is not justified by its cost, the subsidy is all too often withdrawn and the organization dismantled or moved abroad before it can be firmly established.

We propose a simple and effective alternative to subsidies: the government should levy a 7 per cent wholesale tax on the sale of drugs in Canada and then rebate the tax to each firm to the extent of its R&D expenditures in Canada. The firm's R&D expenditures could be in direct support of its own R&D activities, or it could take the form of grants to medical schools, universities or other approved research organizations. Tax monies flowing to the government would be devoted exclusively to the support of R&D in Canada. Since a company that is spending at least 7 per cent of its sales revenue on R&D in Canada would be free of the tax, the multinationals would have a powerful incentive to expand their R&D activities here.

The tax would have little or no impact on product prices, regardless of whether they are demand or cost related. Insofar as prices are demand related, the tax would either reduce profits in Canada or reduce R&D elsewhere in the world, but it would not change the price. Insofar as prices are cost related, neither total cost nor price would increase for firms already spending at least 7 per cent of sales on R&D in Canada or for firms that could usefully increase their R&D

expenditures here to 7 per cent. The tax could have some impact on only the remaining firms.

The critical issue for the overall impact of such a measure is whether or not Canada has the human and institutional resources to carry out useful R&D to the extent of 7 per cent or more of its drug sales. Clearly, the answer is yes, at least in the long run, thus justifying our proposal for inducing multinational firms to increase their R&D in Canada. To avoid a precipitous increase in R&D expenditures that could prove wasteful, the tax might initially be set at 3 per cent and then raised to 7 per cent gradually, over a period of, say, five years.

The tax might fall most heavily on small generic firms, which are not in the business of developing new products, and for which 7 per cent of sales would not support a large enough R&D organization to be profitable. However, it could be argued that such firms should not be relieved of a fair share of the cost of drug innovation. Furthermore, a joint R&D organization could be established and supported by the generic firms, with any new products developed being owned jointly.

Income Taxes

A sore point in how the multinational corporations operate is their ability to avoid income taxes in the countries in which their subsidiaries are located. Through transfer pricing and service charges they are able to allocate income among their subsidiaries at will. With numerous countries offering complete freedom from income taxes, the multinationals have a powerful incentive to reduce their reported income in those countries where it is subject to taxation. A home country can tax a multinational's *worldwide* income, allowing reasonable deductions for taxes paid to other countries, but a subsidiary country such as Canada is at the mercy of the income allocating done by the multinational corporations.

In principle, Canada can look behind these transfer pricing arrangements and levy a tax based on the true income earned by the subsidiary in Canada. In practice, however, the task is quite formidable, and we propose the following solution. The government should calculate the worldwide income of a multinational as a percentage of its worldwide sales and then make the taxable income of its Canadian subsidiary the same percentage of the Canadian sales. For U.S. corporations, the data on worldwide sales and income can be obtained by requiring that their U.S. tax returns be submitted to Canadian tax authorities as a condition for operating in Canada. For corporations in countries where no such tax returns are prepared or where they are unreliable, there are other sources, such as financial statements, that the Canadian government could use.

It may be argued that assigning a multinational's worldwide ratio of income to sales to its Canadian subsidiary is unfair to the extent that the subsidiary carried on only part of the activities that generated the Canadian income. A subsidiary that only sells products discovered and produced abroad does not earn the same profit as a percentage of sales as does the worldwide operation. In such cases, rules might be adopted that make the subsidiary's Canadian income a smaller percentage of sales than the worldwide figure. On the other hand, using the worldwide figure may be a desirable form of discrimination against multinationals that sell products in Canada that are developed and produced elsewhere.

It may be thought that the multinationals could avoid even this taxation if they were to sell their products in Canada through independent wholesalers rather than through their wholly owned subsidiaries. However, marketing activities are so important for the successful sale of their products that multinationals are very reluctant to surrender this vital function to independent wholesalers. Also, the problem of complying with product safety regulations is an additional reason for drug firms to maintain their subsidiaries in Canada. If a multinational should decide to use independent wholesalers, the government could still collect the tax so long as the wholesalers distributed the multinational's brand-name products.

Policies to Reduce Foreign Ownership

Foreign ownership of the Canadian drug industry has not served Canada well. In terms of R&D and production expenditures, we have seen that the performances of a Canadian-owned company (Connaught Laboratories) and two companies that were formerly Canadian owned (Ayerst and Frosst) have been far superior to those of the subsidiaries established in Canada by the multinational drug corporations. For the most part, these subsidiaries have remained primarily sales organizations, with only limited secondary manufacturing. Consequently, the best one can say for the role played by the multinationals in Canada is that they have not removed from Canada the operations of the Canadian companies that they acquired,[14] and in a few instances the subsidiaries they have established here have been expanded beyond the role of a truncated branch plant.

It should be added that the contribution of Connaught (and to a lesser degree Ayerst) cannot be measured solely in narrow economic terms.

Countries, like people, do not live by bread alone. Connaught has contributed significantly to Canada's stature in the world of science and medicine: it has played an important role in the development of insulin, the Salk and Sabine vaccines, and numerous other biological products; its products have been exported throughout the world; it has advised in the development of like organizations in many other countries; and it has provided financial and technical support for the development of scientists (such as Best, Fitzgerald, Defries and Scott) who have achieved worldwide leadership in their fields.[15]

Increased Canadian ownership in our drug industry is highly desirable, and it could be accomplished—it would appear at first glance—in a variety of ways:

- by purchasing either Canadian subsidiaries of multinational corporations or whole foreign companies;
- by expanding generic production, either through existing firms or through the establishment of a crown corporation;
- by the super growth of Canadian firms through the discovery of new products.

However, restoring a significant ownership position is a far more difficult task than preventing its dissipation, as will be seen from the exploration below of these possible courses of action. For this exploration, it will be useful to look first at the history of the CDC Life Sciences, which is a division of the Canada Development Corporation and the only important Canadian drug firm.

CDC Life Sciences

The Canada Development Corporation was established in 1971 by the Canadian government to increase Canadian ownership of industry. The government provided the initial equity capital, and the public provided senior convertible capital. Therefore, the risk during CDC's formative years was borne by the government, but the long-run objective was a significant private ownership of the equity capital, once CDC had demonstrated its profitability. CDC initially made major investments or acquisitions in chemicals and mining, which proved to be—or were made to be—quite profitable, with the result that the company's securities have become very attractive to private investors. CDC has also acquired numerous small, high-risk, high-technology companies, largely in the electronics and life-science industries, and it has put together the largest pool of venture capital in

Canada. This pool consists of equity participation in many small companies with little or no immediate profit prospects, but with interesting growth potential in the long run.

In 1972 CDC acquired Connaught from the University of Toronto, and at the time the purchase was viewed widely as a means whereby CDC could enter the drug industry. The university believed that its mission would be better served by using the funds from the sale to support research in general rather than by continuing to operate Connaught. The university also may have been influenced by Connaught's unattractive prospects at the time. Although the laboratory had been quite profitable over the prior fifty years, having financed its own asset growth and an exceptionally high level of R&D (in all likelihood more than could be justified on purely commercial considerations),[16] still the company had retained all profits and had paid no dividends to the university for support of other activities.

The problem Connaught faced was that its branch of the drug industry (vaccines and other biologicals) was largely concerned with the *prevention* of disease and had been experiencing difficult years, with no relief in sight. The customers for these products were not individuals; they were national or world health organizations. The former favoured domestic suppliers when available, and both were knowledgeable and determined to pay the lowest possible price in a world market where the countries of eastern Europe were competing vigorously. In fact, eastern European prices were so low as to suggest that they were designed to gain entry and prestige in Third World countries.[17] Their vigorous price competition had forced many investor-owned companies in the U.S. and western Europe to contract their activities in—and even to withdraw completely from—the biological branch of the industry. In fact, CDC's purchase of Connaught probably prevented Connaught's severe contraction, and perhaps even its liquidation. CDC may have looked on Connaught as a profitable acquisition for the very long run, but we consider it most unlikely that any privately owned Canadian company (without the CDC's mandate and government financing) would have found Connaught a profitable acquisition at any price.

For several years CDC-Connaught operated at a loss due to depressed markets and to the cost of transforming Connaught from a university-based, research-oriented, nonprofit organization in product lines with no apparent growth potential, into a private-sector, market-oriented company. By the end of the Seventies, however, the transformation had been successfully accomplished. Sales increased from $11.7 million in 1970-71 to $47 million in 1980—due not only to the reorganization of Connaught but also, of course, to inflation. Furthermore, although CDC does not publish income statements for each of the companies in CDC Life Sciences, it would appear from CDC's annual reports that Connaught has become marginally profitable, while at the same time maintaining a high level of R&D. Finally, the attractiveness of Connaught has been enhanced by the spectacular developments in biotechnology (genetic engineering), since Connaught has the manufacturing expertise to develop commercially products that emerge from the research taking place in this new field.

R&D, production and marketing in the biological branch of the pharmaceutical industry (Connaught's area of operation) provides no entry into the much larger, chemically based branch of the industry, where CDC has only acquired a few, very small Canadian companies and Dumex, a medium-sized Danish company that markets its products in Scandinavia, Belgium, the Netherlands and some countries in Asia and Africa. With Dumex representing over one-half of the sales of CDC Life Sciences, the latter has become a medium-sized, highly diversified, pharmaceutical company, with worldwide operations. With the operations of Dumex remaining abroad and with Connaught remaining confined to the biological branch of the industry, CDC Life Sciences cannot be viewed as a world-scale pharmaceutical company *based in Canada*. Furthermore, there is no evidence that CDC Life Sciences looks on generic production as a viable means for building a significant and profitable position in the Canadian pharmaceutical industry.

Perhaps the most important and exciting move by CDC Life Sciences since the acquisition of Connaught is the formation in 1981 of a $100-million joint venture with Labatt and the Province of Ontario to do research in biotechnology.[18] This is by far the largest commitment in Canada to applied R&D in the area of genetic engineering, and CDC Life Sciences has a 50 per cent interest in the operation. What makes this R&D effort particularly promising is that CDC Life Sciences has the financial resources (in CDC) and the production ability (in Connaught) to follow through on the commercial development of any discoveries coming out of this joint venture. Furthermore, CDC Life Sciences is a unique resource for the commerical development in Canada of any discoveries in biotechnology that may take place in the country.

Acquisition Route

Purchasing the Canadian subsidiaries of multinational corporations is not a feasible means of increasing Canadian ownership in the drug industry. The plants themselves are worth little more than the value of their floor space, since the equipment is of little consequence, and the essence of each firm is the combination of its product line (patents and brand names) and the sales organization that maintains its market position. Acquiring the sales organization and the Canadian rights to the product line along with the plant would only make the company a Canadian-owned appendage of a multinational corporation. In addition, the continuing relations between the parent and the Canadian-owned subsidiary regarding the sharing of the revenues on the parent's products would be a financial nightmare.

The acquisition of a medium-sized company located abroad and the transfer of its operations to Canada is also not a practical alternative, since it would be considered an unfriendly act by the foreign government, and in addition, it would drastically reduce the company's value. At best, the operation could be transferred to Canada only gradually through the relative growth of the Canadian operation, making the social as well as the private return on the investment very unattractive. Only the repurchase of Ayerst (and perhaps Frosst) might make sense, since it would provide a Canadian-based presence in the worldwide industry, but Ayerst is now an important component of American Home Products and, undoubtedly, is not for sale.

The above conclusion that an important Canadian presence in the industry cannot be established through the acquisition of a foreign pharmaceutical firm is confirmed by CDC Life Sciences' acquisition of Dumex. That acquisition has not provided—and is not likely to provide—a base for moving into the Canadian pharmaceutical industry. It should be added, though, that the acquisition of Dumex has provided CDC Life Sciences with a worldwide marketing organization that may prove useful in marketing abroad products of other divisions of CDC Life Sciences. For the present, however, Dumex appears to be completely absorbed with the task of making its existing operations more than marginally profitable.

Generic Route

Foreign ownership could be reduced by increasing the generics' share of the market, since a large portion of generic production here is by Canadian firms. Specifically, the two Canadian generic producers of any consequence represent close to 50 per cent of generic production. We can assume then that the measures discussed earlier to eliminate or curb discount competition would increase Canadian ownership simply by increasing generic production. In addition, there are other measures, both provincial and federal and of a conventional nature, that could be used to stimulate the growth of *Canadian* generic producers.[19]

Two other ways whereby Canadian ownership could profitably be increased via the generic route should be noted. One is entry into the industry by a Canadian company with the financial resources of a CDC through the acquisition of a generic producer. The other is a more favourable attitude toward Canadian generic producers on the part of both the cooperative purchasing organizations employed by the pharmacists and the provincial agencies that regulate the marketing of drugs.

However, even though the above measures would reduce the domination of the Canadian market by foreign multinationals, the domination would by no means be eliminated. That would require legislation to eliminate the use of brand names, which would make marketing activities generally ineffective. Unfortunately, this course of action would have a number of undesirable consequences:

- R&D would practically disappear and the industry would lose its high-technology attractiveness;
- the competition would be among a large number of small, *inefficient* producers, so that the competition would actually limit the fall in prices;
- the regulatory problems of ensuring product safety would become quite severe.

On the last point, the large marketing expenditures incurred by a brand-name producer to establish its product constitute a powerful incentive to maintain product quality. With easy entry into the industry and with price the only form of competition, no such inducement to maintain product quality would exist, and the government's regulatory burden would become very onerous.

The problem of inefficiency and product safety caused by having large numbers of small firms could be avoided by creating a crown corporation instead. Since the technology of drug production is simple enough, such a corporation could produce the full range of drugs at costs well below their brand-name prices. However, this solution would require legislation to eliminate brand-name competition, and such legislation in favour of a crown corporation would have serious political implications for our relations with the U.S. and other countries. It could only be justified if the conduct of the firms in the industry became intolerable.

It may be argued that using a crown corporation to eliminate the multinationals would also eliminate the gross profits that finance the R&D that provides immense benefits to Canada. The facts are, though, that prices and R&D in Canada have very little influence on the R&D carried on throughout the world, that the latter determines the new drugs available to Canada, and that Canada can enjoy the benefits of this worldwide R&D without bearing its "fair share" of the cost. Many would view this as too selfish a course of action, feeling that prices in Canada should cover a fair share of the worldwide expenditures on R&D. However, it can also be argued that a fair share of these expenditures should take place in Canada.

Growth Route

The politically acceptable route for increased Canadian ownership in the drug industry would be through the discovery of new products and the consequent super growth of Canadian firms as they exploit these products. However, most new products are discovered in the R&D organizations of large companies, requiring the pre-existence of such organizations in Canada. Although discovery may also take place in university and government laboratories, commercial development requires an enormous investment in refinement, in human testing, and in marketing, and that investment is only economical when carried out by a large company already established in the industry. In the drug industry it is now impossible to build a new firm on a new product. Even if it were possible, a vastly more profitable course of action for the discoverer would be to sell the patent to an existing firm.

The above discussion demonstrates clearly the enormous benefits that can accrue to Canada from the presence here of CDC Life Sciences—not only from the new products it may discover, but also from its ability to develop commercially discoveries that take place elsewhere in Canada. It should be added that the ability of CDC Life Sciences to play this role is enhanced by the operation of the Foreign Investment Review Agency. It is unfortunate that Canada has only this one instrument for expanding its role in the area of life sciences.

Conclusions

We may now draw two major conclusions on increasing Canadian ownership in the pharmaceutical industry: one pessimistic and the other optimistic. The pessimistic conclusion is that a dramatic increase in Canadian ownership is not a feasible goal in the short run, since it would involve unacceptably high costs in relation to the economic benefits obtained. The optimistic conclusion is that *in the long run* increased Canadian ownership is not only feasible but it can benefit Canada in terms of improved employment opportunities and lower consumer prices. This will involve continued support for research and encouragement of the commercial development by CDC Life Sciences (or another Canadian firm) of any discoveries that take place. It will also involve the various policies discussed earlier for expanding generic production by Canadian firms. Finally, it should be noted that our policy recommendations for increasing Canadian ownership in the pharmaceutical industry complement our earlier policy recommendations for improving the performance of multinational subsidiaries in providing Canadians with attractive employment opportunities and reasonable drug prices.

Appendix

Data Sources

This appendix explains the derivation of the data in all but two of the tables of chapters 3 and 4. The first section explains the derivation of the comparative Canadian/American price indices for 1968 and 1976 that are discussed in chapter 3 and that appear in Table 4-3. The subsequent sections are devoted to the income statements and related statistics of the Canadian and American pharmaceutical industries for1968 and 1976, under section headings that are self-explanatory.

Table 4-3: Comparative Price Indices

The price and quantity data in both Canada and the U.S. for the drugs included in our sample were obtained from IMS of Canada Limited, the Canadian subsidiary of a worldwide organization that specializes in the collection of such data for the pharmaceutical industry. Their procedure for a country is to obtain photocopies of all drug invoices from a selected sample of pharmacists in order to compile price information for each drug in terms of dosage form, package size, and supplier. The results are then extrapolated to obtain for each supplier in the country an estimate of its price and quantity sold. IMS is the best available source of such data for Canada and the U.S.

The drugs included in our sample were selected as follows:

- A preliminary sample of drugs was compiled from Ontario's *Drug Benefit Formulary*. This sample was designed to be representative of *the largest selling drugs in each of the major therapeutic classes* in Canada.
- Those drugs that were not also reported in the IMS data for the U.S. were eliminated.
- The remaining drugs were matched for the two countries as to dosage size, and only those drugs for which the most popular dosage size was the same in both countries were retained.

As Table 4-3 shows, a total of 167 drugs could be matched in this manner from the 1968 data and 196 from the 1976 data. Our sample included both prescription and over-the-counter drugs.

For each drug included in the sample, its average price in each country was calculated as follows:

$$P_{xi} = \frac{\sum_j \sum_k Q_{xijk} \, P_{xijk}}{\sum_j \sum_k Q_{xijk}} = \frac{\sum_j \sum_k Q_{xijk} \, P_{xijk}}{Q_{xi}}$$

where Q_{xijk} is the reported quantity in country x, of drug i, in package size j, sold by supplier k; and where P_{xijk} is the reported price in country x, of drug i, in package size j, sold by supplier k. Also, U.S. prices were converted to their Canadian equivalent at the prevailing exchange rate.

Finally, two Canadian/U.S. price indices were computed, one based on quantity weights and the other with equal weight given to each drug. They are, respectively:

$$I_q = \frac{\sum_i Q_{ci} \, P_{ci}}{\sum_i Q_{ci} \, P_{ui}}, \quad \text{and}$$

$$I_e = \frac{1}{N} \sum_{i=1}^{N} \frac{P_{ci}}{P_{ui}},$$

where Q_{ci} and P_{ci} are, respectively, the quantity and the average price in Canada of drug i, and P_{ui} is the price in the U.S. of drug i.

The construction of any price index involves an arbitrary decision regarding the weights to be assigned to each price. For the quantity-weighted index, it might have been considered equally logical to use U.S. quantities as the weights. However, our use of Canadian quantities is appropriate, since our objective is to determine prices in Canada relative to the U.S. for the drugs that Canadians purchased. In choosing between I_q and I_e, the quantity-weighted index places more emphasis on high-volume drugs than on the more specialized, low-volume ones, while the equally weighted index places equal emphasis on both. If prices in Canada relative to the U.S. are lower for high-volume products than for low-volume products, then the quantity-weighted index should give a lower value than the equally weighted index.

One problem in developing the indices should be noted. IMS data was available for both pharmacies and hospitals in Canada but only for pharmacies in the U.S. Our indices were, therefore, computed solely on the basis of pharmacy data. However, since the Canadian data shows that sales of the same drug to hospitals and to pharmacies were made at different prices, it is possible that our comparative price index is biased by the exclusion of hospital data. In both countries hospitals tend to use their high-volume consumption as a bargaining tool to extract price concessions from drug manufacturers, frequently calling for tenders from several suppliers—including generic producers where substitutes are available. However, the generic substitutes made available by compulsory licensing increased the number of products in Canada for which hospitals could obtain lower prices. Consequently, between 1968 and 1976, Canadian/U.S. price ratios should have fallen more for hospitals than for pharmacies, and to the extent that they did, our index understates the relative fall in Canadian prices.

Another possible source of bias in our index worth noting is in the opposite direction. As stated earlier, the sample was weighted in favour of high-volume drugs. Since low-volume drugs were more likely to have gone up in price (they were not made subject to generic competition and they were more likely to have been imported), our weighting somewhat overstates the relative fall in Canadian prices. The large size of the sample, however, limits the extent of the error.

Tables 3-1 and 4-4: Condensed Income Statements

The Canadian data were obtained from Statistics Canada, *Manufacturers of Pharmaceuticals and Medicines* (Ottawa: various years); and from Statistics Canada, *Manufacturing Industries of Canada: Volume I—National and Provincial Areas* (Ottawa: various years). The U.S. data were obtained from the U.S. Census Bureau, *Census of Manufactures* (Washington, D.C.: U.S. Government Printing Office, various years) and from the U.S. Census Bureau, *Annual Survey of Manufacturers* (Washington, D.C.: U.S. Government Printing Office, various years).

The data in Tables 3-1 and 4-4 were derived from the above census data with one exception. The wages paid to production workers are defined to consist of their earnings (as reported by the *Census*) plus an adjustment for the value of their employers' contributions to fringe benefits for them. The U.S. census data include this adjustment, but the Canadian census data do not. We made the adjustment to the Canadian data, using Statistics Canada, *Labour Costs in Canada: Manufacturing, 1968* (Ottawa: 1969), and Statistics Canada, *Labour Costs in Canada: All Industries, 1976* (Ottawa: 1978). The data in these publications were similarly used in Tables 3-4 and 4-7 to adjust the value of salaries paid to management and professional employees for the value of their fringe benefits.

Census data is used for these tables because it is establishment (plant) data rather than enterprise (corporate) data and is, therefore, more accurate. The primary reason for the greater accuracy is that the products produced in a plant typically fall in one industry, and the plant is correctly classified in that industry. Corporate data includes all the establishments owned by a corporation. A corporation that is engaged in the manufacture of pharmaceutical products may have significant secondary involvement in the products of other industries, such as soaps and cleaning compounds or toilet preparations. Corporate data is also less accurate because it includes such extraneous items as interest and dividends received, profits from unincorporated overseas operations, or other extraordinary items that are not always readily segregated from a corporation's manufacturing activities.

An establishment in certain industries may also be engaged in manufacturing products that fall in other industries. This is most unlikely, though, for the pharmaceutical industry, since its special requirements for purity and sterility make it more economical to confine pharmaceutical plants to the manufacture of only pharmaceutical products.

For some of our tables, corporate as well as establishment data must be used, and the accuracy of the data is impaired to the extent that multi-establishment corporations in the pharmaceutical industry also manufacture products that fall in other industries. However, this problem is less acute in the pharmaceutical industry than in most industries, as can be seen from the data in Tables A-1 and A-2 on the distribution of enterprises in the Canadian and American pharmaceutical industries. In both countries, a very large fraction of these enterprises produce only pharmaceuticals. In the U.S. a large fraction of the value added is by pharmaceutical firms that have establishments in other industries, but practically all of those firms are engaged in activities outside the industry to only a very limited degree.

TABLE A-1
SELECTED STATISTICS FOR DIFFERENT TYPES OF PHARMACEUTICAL ENTERPRISES, CANADA, 1968

Type of Enterprise	Number of Enterprises	Number of Establishments	Primary Establishments	Specialization Ratio	Value Added: Manufacturing
Single-industry:					
Single-establishment	129	129	129	100.0	$135.0
Multi-establishment	—	—	—	—	—
Multi-industry	7	24	11	73.7	82.2
Total	136	153	140	90.1	$217.2

Source: Statistics Canada, *Industrial Organization and Concentration in Manufacturing, Mining and Logging Industries, 1968* (Ottawa: 1973).

TABLE A-2
SELECTED STATISTICS FOR DIFFERENT TYPES OF PHARMACEUTICAL ENTERPRISES, UNITED STATES, 1967

Type of enterprise	Number of Enterprises	Number of Establishments	Primary Establishments	Specialization Ratio	Value Added: Manufacturing
Single-industry	879	965	965	100.0	$ 595.2
Multi-industry	44	667	470	70.5	3,046.2
Total	923	1,632	1,435	87.9	$3,641.4

Source: U.S. Census Bureau, *Enterprise Statistics, 1967: Part I—General Report on Industrial Organization* (Washington, D.C.: U.S. Government Printing Office, 1972).

Tables 3-2 and 4-5: Sales and Condensed Income Statements Classified by Resale Products and Products of Own Manufacture

For Canada our classification of sales by resale products and products of own manufacture was obtained as follows. Census data provided (1) sales of manufactured goods, (2) the value of materials used to produce them, (3) revenues from total activity, and (4) the value of materials used in total activity. Included in the difference between (3) and (1) are revenues produced by resale products, the value of depreciable fixed assets produced by own work for own use, revenues from product rentals, and so on. Real property rentals, dividends, interest, et cetera, are excluded. Discussions with Statistics Canada personnel, however, indicated that practically all of the difference between (3) and (1) is due to resale products, and practically all of the difference between (4) and (2) is due to material costs. Consequently, we have attributed the whole of the difference between (3) and (1) and between (4) and (2) to resale products and to material costs, respectively.

For the U.S., sales of resale products and their cost are not given in the *Annual Survey of Manufactures*, but they are given in the *Census of Manufactures*. Data from the latter for 1963, 1967 and 1972 were used to establish trends for both resale products (as a percentage of total sales) and the cost of resale materials (as a percentage of resale sales) in order to interpolate the 1968 figures and extrapolate the 1976 figures.

For Canada our classification of material costs for resale products and products of own manufacture into those of domestic and foreign origin was carried out as follows. Imports of pharmaceutical goods were obtained from Statistics Canada, *Trade of Canada: Imports, Merchandise Trade* (Ottawa: various years). There the imports are classified into two groups—those on which duty is paid and those that enter duty-free. In general, the former are of a class or kind already made in Canada, whereas the latter are not competitive with Canadian production. It seems reasonable to assume that the duty-free items represent imported production materials and that the items on which duty is paid represent goods imported for resale. According to the *Census*, in 1968 the value of imports where duty applies exceeded the value of resale materials by a small amount, and we added the excess to the duty-free imports—reporting the sum as imported production materials. In 1976, on the other hand, the value of imports requiring duty was less than the value of resale materials, in which case we assumed that some resale of domestically produced goods had taken place.

114

Canadian imports of pharmaceutical products, however, seriously understate the industry's import of production materials. The industry is a large importer of organic chemicals, specialized fillers, and packaging materials, and the trade statistics do not classify these imports by the industry to which they are destined. We assumed that such imports were 5 per cent of sales in both 1968 and 1976 for Canada—an arbitrary figure but a conservative one, we believe. Domestic purchases were obtained as a residual by subtracting all imports from total material costs.

For the U.S. our classification of material costs for resale products and products of own manufacture into those of domestic and foreign origin was based on U.S. Department of Commerce, *U.S. General Imports: Schedule A—Commodity By Country*, FT 135 (Washington, D.C.: U.S. Government Printing Office, 1968 and 1976). These trade statistics are somewhat more detailed than the Canadian, with imports being classified in three broad categories: (1) chemicals suitable for medicinal use or as intermediates in the production thereof; (2) medicinal and pharmaceutical products in bulk; and (3) finished pharmaceutical products. We assumed that the first group represents production materials and the second, resale materials. We ignored the third group on the grounds that finished products are most likely imported directly by wholesalers.

The U.S. industry probably receives some imports of organic chemicals, fillers and packaging materials, but the amount is without doubt extremely small. We assumed it was zero in both years. Here, as for Canada, the cost of domestic materials in products of own manufacture was obtained by subtracting imports from total material costs.

Tables 3-3 and 4-6: Employment, Compensation and Productivity of Production Workers

The data in these tables were all obtained from the Canadian *Census* and the U.S. *Annual Survey*, with Canadian wages adjusted to include employer contributions for fringe benefits, as in Tables 3-1 and 4-4.

Tables 3-4 and 4-7: Distribution of Gross Profits

These tables contain the allocation of the gross-profit figures reported in Tables 3-1 and 4-4 to their component accounts. Various sources were used for this purpose as explained below.

Canadian R&D expenditures, broken down into "payroll" and "purchased services," were obtained from two major sources: Statistics Canada, *Industrial Research and Development Expenditures in Canada* (Ottawa: various years); and Statistics Canada, Science Statistics Centre and Ministry of State for Science and Technology, *Research and Development in Canadian Industry* (Ottawa: 1980). We are indebted to Mr. Humphrey Stead of the Science Statistics Centre for making available certain nonconfidential but unpublished data in this area.

"Salary compensation other than R&D" for Canada was obtained as a residual by deducting the R&D payroll figure from "total compensation of salaried employees." The latter is provided by the *Census* and appears in Tables 3-5 and 4-8.

"Non-payroll selling expenses," "purchased business services," and "other overhead costs" were derived from Statistics Canada, *The Input-Output Structure of the Canadian Economy, 1961-1971* (Ottawa: 1977). This was supplemented with more recent statistics obtained directly from Statistics Canada. The percentages of output expended on various types of input were readily classified to the above categories. Our dollar values were obtained by multiplying these percentages by gross sales.

Finally, Statistics Canada, *Corporation Financial Statistics* (Ottawa: various years), was used to estimate the amounts allocated to depreciation, income taxes, and net profits after taxes. First, the ratio of depreciation to sales that is given in the tax statistics was used to compute the amount of depreciation. Secondly, with the pretax profit figure now known, its allocation between income taxes and net profit after taxes could be made by computing the average tax rate from the tax statistics.

The U.S. data for the items in Tables 3-4 and 4-7 were obtained as follows. R&D expenditures, classified as to payroll and purchased services were obtained from National Science Foundation, *Research and Development in Industry, 1968: Technical Notes and Detailed Statistical Tables*, Surveys of Science Resource Series (Washington, D.C.: 1970). A later issue was used for 1976.

"Salary compensation other than R&D" for the U.S. was obtained as a residual by deducting the R&D payroll figure from "total compensation of salaried employees." The latter is shown in Tables 3-5 and 4-8, and its derivation for the U.S. is explained in the following section.

"Non-payroll selling expenses," "purchased business services,"

116

and "other overhead costs" were obtained for the U.S. in a manner similar to that used for Canada. Here, the input-output statistics were obtained from U.S. Department of Commerce, *The Detailed Input-Output Structure of the U.S. Economy, 1972* (Washington, D.C.: U.S. Government Printing Office, 1979). The input-output coefficients for the U.S. were only available for 1963, 1967 and 1972. It was necessary, therefore, to obtain values for 1968 by interpolation and for 1976 by extrapolation.

For the U.S. the tax statistics were obtained from Internal Revenue Service, *Source Book Statistics of Income* (Washington, D.C.: U.S. Treasury Department, various years). The same procedure used for Canada was followed.

Tables 3-5 and 4-8: Employment, Compensation and Sales Per Employee for Salaried Employees

The Canadian statistics for these tables were obtained from the *Census of Manufactures*, with the "total compensation of salaried employees" adjusted to include employer contributions for fringe benefits, as described earlier. For the U.S., the *Census* and *Annual Survey* data on the number of salaried employees and their total compensation at the three-digit level of aggregation (for example, drugs and medicines) include only those persons actually employed *at* a manufacturing plant. Thus, a one-establishment firm, with its head office, R&D facilities, and other ancillary operations all located at the manufacturing plant, will have all its salaried employees listed. On the other hand, a multi-establishment firm, with an independent head office and R&D facilities, will have only those salaried employees physically located at the manufacturing plant reported. Those who are located elsewhere are reported at the two-digit level of aggregation (for example, the chemical industry, which includes drugs and medicines). This means that we had to use other sources to estimate total employment and compensation of salaried employees in the U.S.

Fortunately, the Department of Labor periodically publishes total employment-by-industry figures in U.S. Bureau of Labor Statistics, *Tomorrow's Manpower Needs: Volume IV—The National Industry-Occupational Matrix and Other Manpower Data* (Washington, D.C.: U.S. Department of Labor, various years), where figures for the total number of employees (wage and salary) in drugs and medicines were available for 1960, 1966, 1970 and 1978. Thus, it was possible to establish a trend in employment and to interpolate values for 1968 and 1976. By subtracting the total employment at the establishment level from this figure, we were able to estimate the number of employees at the head office and elsewhere.

The payroll of these salaried employees who are not located at manufacturing plants was estimated as follows. The average compensation figures in the chemical industry for salaried employees at manufacturing plants and for those employed elsewhere were first computed from *Census* data for 1963, 1967 and 1972. In all three years, the latter exceeded the former by about 10 per cent, with a trend toward a slight increase in the difference. We assumed that the difference between these two figures for the chemical industry would also apply to drugs and medicines. The average compensation for salaried employees at manufacturing plants was increased, therefore, by slightly more than 10 per cent to arrive at an estimated average salary for employees at the head office and elsewhere.

Table 3-6: Percentage Distribution of Employees by Type of Occupation

The figures presented here for Canada were obtained from Statistics Canada, 1971 Census of Canada, Volume III, Part 5, *Labour Force: Industries—Industries by Sex, Showing Occupation Major Groups* (Ottawa). For the U.S. the source was *Tomorrow's Manpower Needs,* cited in the section above. The occupational classifications for the two countries were made comparable by means of Statistics Canada, 1971 Census of Canada, Volume I, *Occupational Classification Manual* (Ottawa: 1971).

Tables 3-7 and 4-9: Allocation of Revenues from the Canadian Drug Industry between Canadian and Foreign Recipients

The breakdown of material cost between foreign and domestic recipients was described earlier. The cost of R&D incurred abroad was obtained from the Science Statistics Centre, referred to above. Business services purchased abroad were derived from unpublished but nonconfidential data for 1972 to 1976 that was provided to us by Statistics Canada. Our figure for 1968 was extrapolated from this data. Net profits after taxes accruing to nonresidents were obtained from Statistics Canada, *Corporations and Labour Unions Returns Act: Part 1—Corporations* (Ottawa: various years). All other expenditures in the two tables were by nature incurred in Canada.

Notes

Chapter 1

[1] The bald statement of this view is advanced only by the multinational corporations and their representatives. Somewhat qualified statements may be found in two essays in Charles P. Kindleberger, ed., *The International Corporation* (Cambridge, Mass.: MIT Press, 1970), namely: Harry G. Johnson, "The Efficiency and Welfare Implications of the International Corporation," pp. 35-56; and John H. Dunning, "Technology, United States Investment, and European Economic Growth," pp. 141-76. See also R.B. MacPherson, *Tariffs, Markets and Economic Progress* (Montreal: Copp Clark, 1958). A textbook that presents a sympathetic view of multinational corporations is S.P. Sethi and R.H. Holton, *Management of the Multinationals* (New York: The Free Press, 1974).

[2] Canada, Privy Council, *Foreign Direct Investment in Canada* (Gray Report) (Ottawa: 1972). A summary is in the *Canadian Forum*, 51 (December 1971).

[3] This viewpoint is reflected in the Gray Report and in Canada, Privy Council, *Foreign Ownership and the Structure of Canadian Industry: Report of the Task Force on the Structure of Canadian Industry* (Watkins Report) (Ottawa: 1968). Also see Kari Levitt, *Silent Surrender: The Multinational Corporation in Canada* (Toronto: Macmillan, 1970); and Stephen Hymer, *The International Operations of National Firms: A Study of Direct Foreign Investment* (Cambridge, Mass.: MIT Press, 1976).

[4] This interpretation is developed in W.T. Easterbrook and H.G.J. Aitken, *Canadian Economic History* (Toronto: Macmillan, 1956), pp. 387-94.

[5] This new nationalism is reflected in such developments as the National Energy Program, the Foreign Investment Review Agency, and the Canada Development Corporation.

[6] For a statement of the neoclassical theory of a perfectly competitive system, see Jack Hirshleifer, *Price Theory and Applications* (Englewood Cliffs, N.J.: Prentice-Hall, 1976). Its application to foreign trade is described in R. E. Caves and R. W. Jones, *World Trade and Payments: An Introduction* (Boston: Little, Brown, 1973).

[7] Included in the voluminous literature that advocates free trade for the Canadian manufacturing sector are the following: D. J. Daly, B. A. Keys and E. J. Spence, *Scale and Specialization in Canadian Manufacturing*, Staff Study No. 21 (Ottawa:

119

Economic Council of Canada, 1968); Harry C. Eastman and Stefan Stykolt, *The Tariff and Competition in Canada* (Toronto: Macmillan, 1967); H. E. English, *Industrial Structure in Canada's International Competitive Position: A Study of the Factors Affecting Economies of Scale and Specialization in Canadian Manufacturing*, The Canadian Trade Committee (Montreal: Private Planning Association of Canada, 1964); N. H. Lithwick, *Prices, Productivity, and Canada's Competitive Position*, The Canadian Trade Committee (Montreal: Private Planning Association of Canada, 1967); E. C. West, *Canada-United States Price and Productivity Differences in Manufacturing Industries, 1963*, Staff Study No. 32 (Ottawa: Economic Council of Canada, 1971); R. J. Wonnacott, *Canada's Trade Options* (Ottawa: Economic Council of Canada, 1975); R. J. Wonnacott and Paul Wonnacott, *Free Trade Between the United States and Canada: The Potential Economic Effects* (Cambridge, Mass.: Harvard University Press, 1967); and Economic Council of Canada, *Looking Outward: A New Trade Strategy for Canada* (Ottawa: 1975).

8 B. W. Wilkinson, *Canada in the Changing World Economy* (Montreal: C. D. Howe Research Institute, 1980), p. 76.

9 One of the most comprehensive comparisons of productivity in Canada and the U.S. included 33 industries, of which 25 were in food processing, textiles, wood, or metal products, and only one—dealing with the paint and varnish industry—represented the chemical industries that include pharmaceutical drugs. See J. G. Frank, *Assessing Trends in Canada's Competitive Position: The Case of Canada and the United States* (Ottawa: Conference Board in Canada, 1977), pp. 55-60.

10 Wonnacott and Wonnacott, *Free Trade*. This work was followed in 1975 by Wonnacott, *Canada's Trade Options*, which claimed that the most advantageous state of affairs for Canada would be universal free trade and that the unilateral elimination of the tariff by Canada would be an improvement over the status quo. In the same year the Economic Council of Canada recommended that "every effort be made by Canada to eliminate its own and other countries' trade barriers." See Economic Council of Canada, *Looking Outward*, p. 188.

11 The theoretical basis for this conclusion may be found in M. J. Gordon, "A World Scale National Corporation Industrial Strategy," *Canadian Public Policy*, 4 (Winter 1978), pp. 46-56.

12 D.J. Fowler, "*A Comparison of the Performance of Canadian and U.S. Manufacturing and Mining Industries*" (Ph.D. thesis, University of Toronto, 1976).

13 A. E. Safarian, *Foreign Ownership of Canadian Industry* (Toronto: McGraw-Hill, 1966).

14 The studies published by the Science Council of Canada on the low level of R&D in Canada include the following: Science Council of Canada, *Innovation in a Cold Climate: The Dilemma of Canadian Manufacturing*, Report No. 15 (Ottawa: 1971); A. J. Cordell, *The Multinational Firm, Foreign Direct Investment and Canadian Science Policy*, Special Study No. 22 (Ottawa: Science Council of Canada, 1972); P. L. Bourgault, *Innovation and the Structure of Canadian Industry*, Special Study No. 23 (Ottawa: Science Council of Canada, 1972); and J. N. H. Britton and J. M. Gilmour, *The Weakest Link: A Technological Perspective on Canadian Industrial Underdevelopment*, Background Study No. 43 (Ottawa: Science Council of Canada, 1978).

[15] Wilkinson, *Canada*, pp. 59-80.

[16] John J. Shepherd, *The Transition to Reality: Directions for Canadian Industrial Strategy* (Ottawa: Canadian Institute for Economic Policy, 1980).

[17] See Table 2-6.

Chapter 2

[1] Wyndham Davies, *The Pharmaceutical Industry: A Personal Study* (Oxford: Pergamon Press, 1967), p. 1.

[2] The historical information was obtained from three major sources: Harry F. Dowling, *Medicines for Man* (New York: Alfred A. Knopf, 1970); Barrie G. James, *The Future of the Pharmaceutical Industry to 1990* (London: Associated Business Programmes, 1977); and Tom Mahomy, *The Merchants of Life* (New York: Harper and Brothers, 1959).

[3] Dowling, *Medicines*, p. 27.

[4] Ibid., p. 40.

[5] A useful summary of the impact of U.S. regulations on the industry is provided in Jerome E. Schnee, "Government Control of Therapeutic Drugs: Intent, Impact and Issues," in Cotton M. Lindsay, ed., *The Pharmaceutical Industry* (Toronto: John Wiley and Sons, 1978), pp. 9-22.

[6] The theory concerning the influence of price inelasticity, patent law, and government regulation on the development of the drug industry's structure is well known, and it is summarized in Peter Temin, "Technology, Regulation, and Market Structure in the Modern Pharmaceutical Industry," *The Bell Journal of Economics*, 10 (Autumn 1979), pp. 429-46.

[7] Davies, *Pharmaceutical Industry*, p. 38.

[8] Temin, "Technology," p. 431.

[9] James, *The Future*, p. 25.

[10] See Charles Levinson, *The Multinational Pharmaceutical Industry* (Geneva: International Federation of Chemical and General Workers' Union, 1973), p. 21.

[11] Recently, Puerto Rico and Ireland, both offering very attractive tax environments, have been favoured sites for fine chemical production. See "The U.S. Pharmaceutical Industry in Puerto Rico," and "The U.S. Health Care Industry in Ireland," both published by the Chase Manhattan Bank, c. 1976.

[12] Vernon A. Mund, "The Return on Investment of the Innovative Pharmaceutical Firm," in Joseph D. Cooper, ed., *The Economics of Drug Innovation* (Washington, D.C.: Center for the Study of Private Enterprise, The American University, 1970), pp. 125-38.

[13] See W. Duncan Reekie and Michael H. Weber, *Profits, Politics and Drugs* (New York: Holmes and Meier, 1979), pp. 7-8.

[14] Christopher M. Martin, "Reliability in Product Performance in an Innovative Environment," in Cooper, *Economics*, pp. 63-82.

[15] Ronald W. Lang, *The Politics of Drugs* (Farnborough: Saxon House, D.C. Heath Ltd., 1974), p. 31, provides an excellent example of this problem of nomenclature:

"Chemical Name: The hydrochloride of 7-chloro-4-dimenthylaminio-1, 4, 4a, 5,

5a, 6, 11, 12a - octahydro - 3, 6, 10, 12, 12a - pentahydroxy - 6 - methyl - 1, 11 - dioxo - 2 - napthacene carboxamide.

"Generic Name: chlortetracycline HCL.

"Trade Name: Aureomycin (registered trade name Cyanamid)."

[16] See, among others, Harry C. Eastman and Stefan Stykolt, *The Tariff and Competition in Canada* (Toronto: Macmillan, 1967); and Raymond Vernon, *Sovereignty at Bay: The Multinational Spread of U.S. Enterprises* (New York: Basic Books, 1971).

[17] In some instances chemical companies in Canada were able to take advantage of the same tariff provisions, thereby replacing imported sources with domestic fine chemicals. These opportunities were generally rare, since they usually required the cooperation of the customer drug company.

[18] *A Profile* (Ottawa: Pharmaceutical Manufacturers Association of Canada, 1980).

[19] Connaught Laboratories was established in 1914 in the Department of Hygiene at the University of Toronto in order to meet the country's public health needs for vaccines and to strengthen medical research at the university. Its subsequent growth was stimulated by its important contributions to the improvement of insulin and the development of other biological products.

[20] *1970 Report of the Committee to Examine the Patent System and Patent Law* (Banks Committee), as quoted in Lang, *Politics of Drugs*, p. 27.

[21] Statistics Canada, *Industrial Organization and Concentration in the Manufacturing, Mining and Logging Industries, 1968* (Ottawa: 1973).

[22] Canada, Restrictive Trade Practices Commission, *Report Concerning the Manufacture, Distribution and Sale of Drugs* (Ottawa: Department of Justice, 1963), Appendix Q, p. 247.

[23] Ibid., p. 526. Needless to say, the industry mounted a spirited defence against this and other attacks on the patent system and industry practices through its trade association, the Pharmaceutical Manufacturers Association of Canada. An excellent blow-by-blow description of these battles is given in Lang, *Politics of Drugs*.

[24] As quoted in Lang, *Politics of Drugs*, p. 190.

[25] As quoted in Ibid., pp. 306-9.

[26] For a more complete description of the sequence leading to the passage of Bill C-102, see Ibid., pp. 243-52.

[27] Ibid., p. 14.

[28] Ibid., chapters 9 and 11.

[29] A number of developing countries have considered legislation very similar to that adopted in Canada. See Peter O'Brien, *Trademarks, the International Pharmaceutical Industry, and the Developing Countries*, Occasional Papers No. 63 (The Hague: Institute of Social Studies, 1977).

Chapter 3

[1] Canada, Restrictive Trade Practices Commission, *Report Concerning the Manufacture, Distribution and Sale of Drugs* (Ottawa: Department of Justice, 1963), Appendix Q, pp. 203-17. The drugs included in this sample were not selected to be

122

representative of those consumed in Canada, and the prices used were list prices.

2 Bohumir Pazderka, "Promotion and Competition in the Canadian Prescription Drug Industry" (Ph.D. thesis, Queen's University, 1976).

3 This 11.6 per cent understates the true volume of resale sales in Canada, since the packaging of a drug product in Canada, including merely labeling it for reshipment to pharmacists, apparently qualifies the product for the designation, "Made in Canada."

4 Total imports were 11.5 per cent of sales; net of the tariff (12.4 per cent on average), they were 10.1 per cent of sales; and their production cost with a 50 per cent gross margin was 5.1 per cent of sales. A gross margin of 50 per cent is a conservative estimate, because it is smaller than the implicit margin on the sale of resale products to Canadian subsidiaries.

5 We have been told that higher standards of quality control in Canada than in the U.S. also tend to make output per worker lower in Canada.

6 We have no data on Ayerst, a Canadian firm that became a foreign subsidiary through acquisition, but our knowledge of the company suggests that it accounted for more than 25 per cent of exports. Hence, the exports by subsidiaries established here were less than half the total and quite negligible.

7 If R&D in Canada is a form of featherbedding, one might wonder who bears the cost. The consumer would bear the cost if the featherbedding raised prices in Canada, but our comparative data suggest that prices are not higher in Canada than in the U.S. Hence, the R&D cost reduces the profits of foreign parents. The employment provided is then a net benefit to Canada, even if the R&D is useless.

8 We are indebted to Dr. J. K. W. Ferguson for providing us with this and other data on Connaught Laboratories for the years prior to its acquisition by Canada Development Corporation. Similar data from firms in the private sector would have substantially increased the detail, accuracy and usefulness of our results.

9 A study of R&D expenditures that covered all industries found that Canadian-owned firms generally do more R&D than foreign subsidiaries, but the latter are more successful in getting their R&D subsidized by the Canadian government. See D. G. McFetridge, *Government Support of Scientific Research and Development: An Economic Analysis* (Toronto: University of Toronto Press, 1977).

10 See Pharmaceutical Manufacturers Association of Canada, *Background Information on the Canadian Pharmaceutical Manufacturing Industry* (Ottawa: October 1979), Appendix 7(E). The PMAC estimated that selling expenses were 30 per cent of sales in 1964. The difference between their figure and our 20 per cent may be due to: (1) their having divided selling expenses by sales of products of own manufacture instead of by total sales; (2) their having included several small items of expense that we excluded; and (3) the reduction of selling expenses between 1964 and 1968 in response to various studies which noted and criticized its very high level.

11 An informative discussion of selling effort in the industry may be found in R. S. Bond and David F. Lean, *Sales Promotion and Product Differentiation in Two Prescription Drug Markets* (Washington, D.C.: U.S. Federal Trade Commission, 1977).

12 With U.S. production costs 32.4 per cent of sales (Table 3-2), and with transfer prices 82.5 per cent of sales on resale products, the pretax net profit to the parent on

123

resale products was about 50 per cent of sales. These sales were 11.6 per cent of total sales, providing the parents with a profit equal to about 5.8 per cent of total sales. A similar calculation for the 6.5 per cent of Canadian sales spent on the import of drugs to be used in products of own manufacture results in 2.8 per cent.

13 Of course, we are referring here to the prices charged Canadian pharmacists. The prices charged consumers depended, in addition, on the gross-profit margins of the pharmacists.

14 This may be an overstatement of the expenditures in Canada, due to the way the figure is obtained. If the foreign component of an expenditure account is reported to the government and published, it is deducted from the total expenditure for the account. Such expenditures may be underreported—not overreported—or they may not be reported at all. In other words, if companies were to report domestic instead of foreign expenditures, they would be deducted from the total, and they would be understated in some measure.

Chapter 4

1 See, for example, W. Duncan Reekie, *The Economics of the Pharmaceutical Industry* (London: Macmillan Press, 1975), chapter 5.

2 The discussion that follows is confined to the Ontario legislation on product selection. In Quebec and certain other provinces, the legislation is somewhat different. Over all ten provinces, the legislation ranges from none in Alberta to what is, in effect, compulsory selection of the least-cost product by the pharmacist in Saskatchewan.

3 They were Apotex, Frank W. Horner, ICN and Novopharm; of these, two are Canadian owned.

4 See Bohumir Pazderka, "Promotion and Competition in the Canadian Prescription Drug Industry" (Ph.D. thesis, Queen's University, 1976), who cites the *Globe and Mail*, 28 October 1972, as the source of his information.

5 Thomas K. Fulda and Paul F. Dickens III, "Controlling the Cost of Drugs: The Canadian Experience," *Health Care Financing Review*, 1 (Fall 1979), pp. 55-64.

6 Paul K. Gorecki and Andrew B. Klymchuk, "Government Intervention, Regulation, and Competition in the Prescription Drug Market in Canada, 1969-1979" (Paper presented at the Annual Meeting of the Canadian Economics Association, Montreal, June 1980).

7 *Globe and Mail*, 7 February 1980, reported the conviction of Hoffmann-La Roche under the Combines Investigation Act for trying to eliminate competition in this way.

8 Following the completion of this study, another study of drug prices appeared: Paul K. Gorecki, *Regulating the Price of Prescription Drugs in Canada: Compulsory Licensing, Product Selection, and Government Reimbursement Programmes*, Technical Report No. 8 (Ottawa: Economic Council of Canada, 1981). Gorecki's conclusion was that drug prices in Canada have been reduced substantially by the government's competition policy, based on a comparison of the actual drug bill in each province with *his* estimate of what the drug bill would have been without the competition policy. He did not compare price movement in Canada with that in the U.S.

[9] See "Closing In on Puerto Rico's Tax Haven," *Business Week* (22 May 1978), p. 154.

[10] This data on Puerto Rico illustrates the devastating consequences for a country of leaving the control of multinational corporations to the "free play of market forces."

[11] See Pharmaceutical Manufacturers Association of Canada, *Background Information on the Canadian Pharmaceutical Manufacturing Industry* (Ottawa: October 1979), Appendix 6.

[12] Ibid., Appendix 7, Section E. See also the quarterly publication of the Pharmaceutical Manufacturers Association of Canada, *Insight*, 1 (January 1981), p. 4.

Chapter 5

[1] The Pharmaceutical Manufacturers Association reported that in 1978 total sales of products under compulsory license were $56.4 million, but only $10.0 million were by firms that had obtained compulsory licenses. Since the latter firms charge lower prices, it follows that their sales were a larger fraction of the total sales on a quantity basis than they were on a dollar basis. Furthermore, the $56.4-million total was a small fraction of the sales of all pharmaceutical products, because production under compulsory license was taking place on only eighteen products. See Pharmaceutical Manufacturers Association of Canada (PMAC), *Background Information on the Canadian Pharmaceutical Manufacturing Industry* (Ottawa: October 1979), Appendix 6, Attachment B.

[2] See Paul K. Gorecki, *Regulating the Price of Prescription Drugs in Canada: Compulsory Licensing, Product Selection, and Government Reimbursement Programmes*, Technical Report No. 8 (Ottawa: Economic Council of Canada, 1981), pp. 136-37. He reported that for eight drugs under compulsory license in 1980, the list prices in the Ontario *Drug Benefit Formulary* averaged almost *twice* (192.5 per cent, to be exact) their actual cost to the pharmacist. Consequently, the implementation in Ontario of legislation authorizing product selection now serves the pharmacist and the multinational producer, but not the consumer or the generic producer. We understand that Ontario is concerned with this problem.

[3] Consider a product with a sales price of $10.00 and a production cost of $4.00. Also, let the Canadian tariff and income tax be, respectively, 10 per cent and 50 per cent. Then, an increase in the transfer price from $4.00 to $5.00 would raise the tariff paid to Canada on the product by $.10. However, the increase in the transfer price also would reduce the profit reported in Canada by $1.00, reducing the income tax paid to Canada by $.50. Hence, with a zero income tax in the country of export, the $1.00 increase in the transfer price would reduce taxes paid *in total* by $.40. For more on the subject of transfer pricing, see G. F. Mathewson and G. D. Quirin, *Fiscal Transfer Pricing in Multinational Corporations* (Toronto: University of Toronto Press, 1980).

[4] Ciba-Geigy was reported to have withdrawn a research program from Canada on new therapeutic uses for a drug because a compulsory license was obtained on the drug. See *Globe and Mail*, 18 December 1979, p. 4. Similar decisions by other firms, including the transfer of a research division out of Canada, have been reported.

5 However, with the development of electronic computers it is increasingly possible to make the location of a firm's accounting and other information-processing activities independent of the location of its primary activities. With the output of the information-processing activity transferred to a central location, management decisions are also centralized, and the managerial personnel located in the subsidiary plant is reduced correspondingly.

6 The U.S. has extremely strict standards—so strict, in fact, that there is a lag of time from one to five years between the introduction of a drug into the U.K. (or some other western European country) and the U.S. Hence, acceptance by the U.S. could be used as a standard—if the primary concern is avoidance of harmful drugs. Otherwise, acceptance by any one of a small number of countries could be the standard.

7 The rules governing the initial tests of a new drug to determine whether or not it is harmful are more stringent and costly in the U.S. than in Canada. Therefore, the rules favour the use of Canada for this stage of the clinical testing.

8 See Canadian Drug Manufacturers Association, "Position Paper on the Subject Matter of Changing the Pharmaceutical Patent Laws and Its Impact" (Scarborough, Ont.: 1 November 1979).

9 Ronald W. Lang, *The Politics of Drugs* (Farnborough: Saxon House, D. C. Heath Ltd., 1974), pp. 249-52.

10 PMAC, *Background Information*, Appendix 6.

11 In order to speed up the introduction of new drugs into Canada, the period of exclusive use of a drug should begin as soon as the patent is granted by Canada and not at a later date when the product is actually introduced. However, this need not reduce the period of exclusive sale very much, since the considerable time period between the application for and the granting of a patent is available for developing and marketing the product.

12 The records already required of the pharmacist would make such legislation relatively easy to enforce. The price to the pharmacist would be the price to any wholesaling organization in which the pharmacist has an interest.

13 Actually, Saskatchewan's policy is even more drastic. In effect it does the procurement for the pharmacist, since the pharmacist is required to buy the product from the firm that quotes the lowest price to the province.

14 Ayerst is a notable exception in one respect. The R&D organization for the development of new products that serves Ayerst worldwide is located in Canada, and this organization has grown substantially since the acquisition of Ayerst by American Home Products. On the other hand, Ayerst's production in Canada is probably less than 10 per cent of its worldwide production and practically all of its R&D for human testing of new products is done abroad.

15 See Connaught Medical Research Laboratories and Connaught Laboratories Limited, *59th Annual Report, 1971-1972* (Willowdale, Ont.); and J. K. W. Ferguson, "The Story of Poliomyelitis Vaccines," *Canadian Journal of Public Health*, 55 (May 1964), pp. 183-90.

16 In 1970-71, the last full year before its purchase by CDC, Connaught had a gross margin of 50 per cent on its sales of $11,681,768. Its profit net of all expenses but R&D was 31.1 per cent of sales, and after R&D it was 11.2 per cent.

[17] The price of antipolio vaccine had fallen to the point where its cost-per-dosage was below that of over-the-counter headache medications.

[18] It was reported in the *Globe and Mail* (24 February 1981), p. B9, and in Canada Development Corporation, *First Quarter Report, 1981*.

[19] On the provincial level, giving preference to Canadian firms in hospital purchases would be beneficial. On the federal level, the approval of new drugs can be used as a powerful instrument for helping national firms. In many countries (including the U.S. and Japan), the approval of a drug for which a substitute is already on the market is subject to long delays and very demanding tests if the applicant is a subsidiary of a foreign multinational.

The Canadian Institute for Economic Policy Series

The Monetarist Counter-Revolution: A Critique of Canadian Monetary Policy 1975-1979
Arthur W. Donner and Douglas D. Peters

Canada's Crippled Dollar: An Analysis of International Trade and Our Troubled Balance of Payments
H. Lukin Robinson

Unemployment and Inflation: The Canadian Experience
Clarence L. Barber and John C. P. McCallum

How Ottawa Decides: Planning and Industrial Policy-Making 1968-1980
Richard D. French

Energy and Industry: The Potential of Energy Development Projects for Canadian Industry in the Eighties
Barry Beale

The Energy Squeeze: Canadian Policies for Survival
Bruce F. Willson

The Post-Keynesian Debate: A Review of Three Recent Canadian Contributions
Myron J. Gordon

Water: The Emerging Crisis in Canada
Harold D. Foster and W. R. Derrick Sewell

The Working Poor: Wage Earners and the Failure of Income Security Policies
David P. Ross

Beyond the Monetarists: Post-Keynesian Alternatives to Rampant Inflation, Low Growth and High Unemployment
Edited by David Crane

The Splintered Market: Barriers to Interprovincial Trade in Canadian Agriculture
R. E. Haack, D. R. Hughes and R. G. Shapiro

The New Protectionism: Non-Tariff Barriers and Their Effects on Canada
Fred Lazar

The above titles are available from:

James Lorimer & Company, Publishers
Egerton Ryerson Memorial Building
35 Britain Street
Toronto M5A 1R7, Ontario